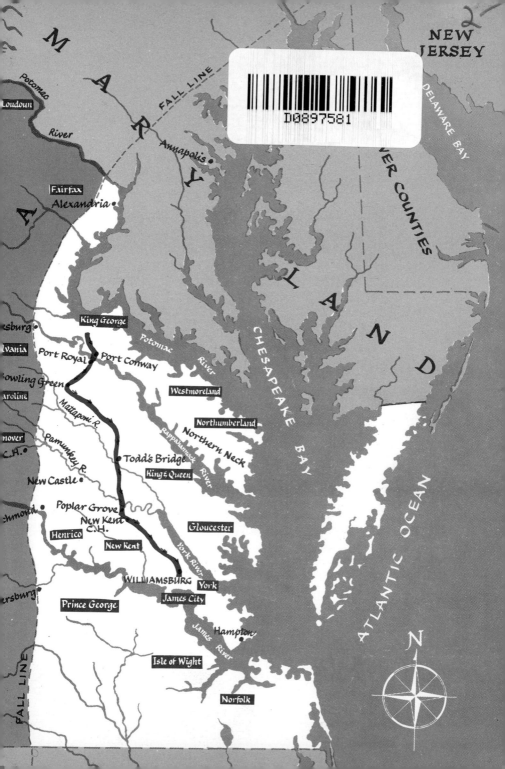

SEAT OF EMPIRE

Williamsburg in America Series

I

The first in a series of popular histories
of Williamsburg and Tidewater Virginia in
the eighteenth century.

Seat of Empire

THE POLITICAL ROLE OF
EIGHTEENTH-CENTURY
WILLIAMSBURG

by

Carl Bridenbaugh

NEW EDITION
Williamsburg, Virginia
Published by COLONIAL WILLIAMSBURG
Distributed by HENRY HOLT & COMPANY, INC., *New York*

For
Douglass Adair

PREFACE

This new edition of *Seat of Empire* has provided the opportunity for me to correct some deficiencies in the original of 1950. I hope that most of them have been removed. For their patience and courtesy in drawing slips and mis-statements to my attention, I desire to thank especially David J. Mays, the Research Department of Colonial Williamsburg, and Roberta Bridenbaugh. I also take a sly satisfaction in having myself discovered some slips which eluded the attention of these friends.

Since this little book appeared in 1950, a number of important volumes about Virginia in the eighteenth century have been published; they are noted in the revised and expanded *Note on the Sources* and *Suggestions for Further Reading*. It is a real pleasure to recommend these works as much for their literary charm as for their authoritativeness as history.

CARL BRIDENBAUGH

Berkeley, California
17 December 1957

CONTENTS

ILLUSTRATIONS

SEAT OF EMPIRE

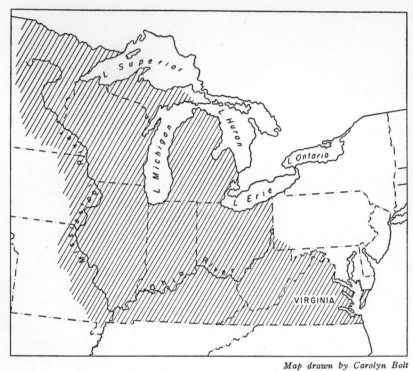

Map drawn by Carolyn Bolt

VIRGINIA'S CLAIMS TO EMPIRE, 1776

Map showing claims as far west as the Mississippi River

1

THE OLD DOMINION, 1750-1779

Virginia is Bounded by the Great Atlantic Ocean to the East, by North Carolina to the South, by Maryland and Pennsylvania to the North, and by the South Sea to the West, including California.
—THOMAS LEE TO THE BOARD OF TRADE, 1750

As land-hungry Virginians like Thomas Lee faced westward from their Tidewater lands in 1750 and succeeding years, the sheer immensity of the extent of the Old Dominion fired their imaginations and supplied a fillip to their activities. Expansion was in the air. All the people of the colony, Tidewater Tuckahoe and back-country Cohee alike, were infected with the virus of empire building. Although we may smile at Colonel Lee's inflated limits, we must admit that east of the Mississippi River Virginia could lay valid claims to a princely domain of 359,480 square miles—a territory three times the size of King George's British Isles! As it existed at the close of the War for Independence, the commonwealth was still larger than all of New England with Delaware tossed in for good measure.

In population as well as size Virginia led all the colonies. It contained nearly twice as many inhabitants in 1776 as Massachusetts, or Pennsylvania, or Maryland, or North Carolina. The Old Dominion's population—white and black, free and slave—was equal to five-sixths of that of New England, and it composed one-fifth of all the people in the colonies.

By the standards of the eighteenth century this oldest, largest, and most populous colony was properly regarded by Britons as the prime link in the great chain of empire. It furnished the Mother Country with a valuable and much needed staple—tobacco—and in return absorbed ever increasing quantities of British manufactures. Unwavering loyalty to the king was the constant boast of Virginians, who took pardonable pride in the remarkable stability of their society and of their government.

As early as 1700 a pattern of life had been established which made Virginia throughout the century, like Connecticut, a land of steady habits. Verily, her political history before 1750 makes dull reading! No rebellion broke out after Bacon's fiasco of 1676; no foreign enemy ever crossed her boundaries; no rift in the social fabric ever threatened the security of the colony's ruling class.

2

TRAINING THE RULING CLASS

On the Plantation. Let us begin with the people. Tidewater Virginia presented the unusual spectacle of a whole society devoting its energies to the production of a single crop—"that chopping herbe of hell, tobacco." Cultivation of the soil absorbed the attention of nearly all the inhabitants—rich, middling, and poor, white or black—and nearly all lived on some kind of a farm. That in the whole colony there was no town of consequence astonished visitors in these years. The essence of eighteenth-century Virginia was its *rural quality*. And yet, with a few significant exceptions, most colonial Americans were farmers and rustic in their outlook. What was it then that made Virginia's society different? What was there about the Old Dominion that produced within the space of half a century a galaxy of statesmen who, for sagacity, ability, courage, political insight, and absence of provincialism, could challenge any other country or period of history to produce their equals? The answer, in all probability, may be discovered in the plantation way of life and in the system of government that was evolved to meet the needs of this society.

The plantation differentiated Virginia agriculture from that of other communities in old England or the Northern and Middle colonies. The plantation made the Chesapeake society unique. Unlike the traditional American farm, a tobacco estate was virtually a little society in itself. Out of the thousands of acres owned by well-to-do planters, only small areas were actually cleared and under cultivation at one time; most of their lands were still forest. Moreover each large holding was usually divided into several units in order to secure more efficient production: one would contain the "mansion house" where dwelt the owner and his family; others, similarly composed, were operated by overseers or leased by white tenant farmers.

Each unit, or "quarter," had its gang of ten to thirty slaves who performed the heavy work in the fields or at the barns and outbuildings. Contrary to commonly accepted belief, the number of Negroes seldom reached three hundred, even on very large plantations; throughout the whole Tidewater region the average planter owned only eight or ten slaves. Rounding out the population of the plantation were a few white indentured servants, who customarily performed the tasks requiring highly skilled artisans, though here and there one found a "country-born" slave possessing some facility at a trade.

Among the great plantations of Virginia was Nomini Hall, Potomac River seat of Councilor Robert Carter. As the visitor approached it, either by boat up Nomini Creek or by carriage down the long lane impressively flanked by towering poplars, this great estate resembled nothing so much as a tiny village set down in an area carved from the surrounding woodlands. The great mansion of the type so well known to the modern tourist achieved its commanding appearance from the many dependent buildings clustered around it. Four structures—the brick schoolhouse, the washhouse, the coach house, and the stable—formed a square of which the mansion was the center. Stretching westward from the great house were the kitchen, bakehouse, dairy, storehouse, and other small buildings which created the illusion of "a little handsome street." Near the tobacco and corn fields, behind a row of trees which screened them from the main quadrangle, were the rude cabins in which the slaves were quartered.

Perhaps a hundred and fifty souls, black and white, comprised the community at Nomini Hall. Its owner, Robert Carter, presided over this large "family" like some patriarch out of the Old Testament. By virtue of his planning and management—his rule, if you will—the yearly endeavors of the community were a success or a failure. He determined the lands to be cultivated each season, what crops should be planted, how many hogs should be raised, and every other activity on the plantation. It was he who arranged for shipment and sale of the crops when they were harvested, and it was he who made the outside purchases necessary for the little village throughout the coming year. The coopers who fabricated the tobacco casks, the smiths who forged the ironwork and shod the horses, as well as the miller who ground the corn and wheat at Nomini Creek dam—all came under his direct surveillance. He also had to look after the health and clothing of his Negro workers. Over his slaves he virtually enjoyed by law the power of life and death; his white servants were virtually serfs until the expiration of their indentures; his tutors, overseers, clerks, and other white employees were subject to his control and to the plantation routine and discipline. In consequence, the management of a plantation called for something more than mere business acumen or a knowledge of current agricultural methods.

Such a plantation was in reality a tiny, practically self-sufficient society. Mere listing of the quantities consumed by Robert Carter's dependents for the single year 1773 causes astonishment: "27,000 Lb. of Pork, and Twenty Beeves, 550 Bushels of Wheat, besides Corn—4 Hogsheads of Rum and 150 Gallons of Brandy." This society existed, for the most part, little influenced by the outside world. A man could live a long time on an estate like Nomini Hall without becoming aware of the colonial government at Williamsburg, let alone that of His Majesty the King in London.

Nowhere did the eighteenth century provide a more thorough schooling in the management of practical affairs and in the handling of people than on these Tidewater plantations where young Virginians were reared. Early did they develop an awareness of their privileged status; early did they acquire the habit of command. They came into manhood prepared and expecting to rule; it was a birthright bred in their bones and nourished on plantation fare. These traits were, moreover, nicely blended with a formal education in the classical tradition at the plantation school. Though they lived amid rural surroundings, the Virginia gentry displayed a striking urbanity; they were never rustics. To reach maturity in one of these little tobacco societies was to be exposed to a superb elementary training in the difficult art of governing people. One must seek the genesis of the great Virginians of the Revolutionary Era on the plantation; two indispensable crops were there produced: tobacco and leaders.

A PLANTATION

Mount Vernon, the seat of George Washington

A TIDEWATER MANSION
Sabine Hall, home of Landon Carter

A TIDEWATER MANSION
Mount Airy, owned by the Tayloe family

Here the very conditions of life forced upon gentlemen a careful cultivation of those arts so essential to men who propose to lead others—the outward appearance of a leader, an erect bearing, horsemanship, an easy dignity, self-assurance sometimes verging on arrogance, and that prime capacity of reaching decisions quickly.

Born to rule, reared to rule, the generality of these men—as Francis Walker Gilmer, a leading literary figure of Jefferson's day, readily admitted—acquired their culture and learning from conversation rather than from books. Although the majority of the planters were a highly sociable folk who had developed conversation and the external graces to a fine art and who regarded the outdoor life of action as the only good life, the best of these barons of the Tidewater also passed much of their time in reading. Few men of their day were better informed than Virginians on such subjects as history and politics. In Virginia, remarked the observant Duc de La Rochefoucauld-Liancourt, "a taste for reading is more prevalent among the gentlemen of the first class than in any other part of America, but the common people are, perhaps, more ignorant than elsewhere." Some of this first class assembled libraries whose contents included the wisdom of the ages upon the important subject of government. On their shelves were the standard works of Plutarch, Harrington, Sidney, Locke, and the rest, well worn from much reading. For them this study became a necessity, and in their greatest statesmen we perceive immediately the noteworthy combination of the active and the practical with the scholarly and the contemplative that is so refreshingly startling upon first encounter and a matter for amazement and admiration thereafter. Ruling over their own acres was their first lesson in statesmanship; the plantation was their primer of politics.

In the middle of the eighteenth century, perhaps less than one hundred families were seated on plantations in Tidewater Virginia like the one at Nomini Hall. This group formed a parochial aristocracy whose ranks were apparently nearly as difficult to enter as those of the English gentry. For over half a century "gentlemen of the best families and fortunes" had been consciously coalescing into an exclusive ruling class based principally upon the possession of great tracts of land. In part they achieved their desire to perpetuate their families and their power by legal enactments requiring their estates to descend to their eldest sons, who in turn were forbidden to alienate any inherited lands. These were the famous laws of *primogeniture* and *entail*. The ranks of the gentry were further consolidated by carefully planned intermarriages among the great families, since in good eighteenth-century fashion family plans always took precedence over dictates of the heart. The fruits of these arrangements forcibly struck all visitors: "an aristocratical spirit and principle is very prevalent in the laws, policy and manners of this Colony," observed Josiah Quincy, Jr., of Boston, while on a tour of the seaboard in 1773.

Thus privileged by law and carefully selected—one almost says bred—through intermarriage, these Virginians wore an air of assurance and pride of place, exhibited a haughtiness and condescension toward their inferiors, and studiously cultivated the attitudes of leaders—characteristics all of an aristocratic order. Such qualities prevailed among the patrician families of the Old Dominion—Burwells, Byrds, Carters, Corbins, Fitzhughs, Harrisons, Lees, Ludwells, Nelsons, Pages, Randolphs, Robinsons, Tayloes, and their kin. These people were not aristocrats on the make; they were already made, and they and the rest of Virginia knew and admitted it.

The luxuriously furnished great plantation houses that once studded the banks of the Potomac, the Rappahannock, the York, and the James combined with an elaborate elegance of dress on the part of the residents to keep the leading Virginia families in a constant state of emulation with each other. These were their badges of distinction. Regardless of the costs, Tidewater grandees steadily increased their votive offerings to the cult of magnificence. Ostentation was intended to impress— and it did. Dazzled by the conspicuous baronial splendor of the great families of the plantation country, a traveler of the 1760's exclaimed: "In most articles of life a great Virginia planter makes a greater show and lives more luxuriously than a country gentleman in England, on an estate of three or four thousand pounds a year."

Perennially writers emphasize the close resemblance of Tidewater Virginia to the country life of old England. The Chesapeake and Atlantic highways, as well as the tobacco trade, they assert, bound the planters irrevocably to the Mother Country, and, moreover, the Virginians themselves voluntarily, nay eagerly, sought, as John Donne had said, "to make this land . . . the suburbs of the Old World." From a cursory glance this contention seems true. There was much indeed about the tobacco plantation that resembled the seat of an English squire. Much more important than the fact itself was the belief of Virginians that they were living in the manner of the English squirearchy.

Actually these men were more American than they knew. Not until threats of the application of naked power by the British authorities came in the 1760's did they begin to sense how far they had diverged from the English norm in thought and in deed. In 1765 Virginians sincerely protested their loy-alty to their king—*but it was a loyalty of their own defining*. Loyalty to their own class and tradition—to Virginia, as they would have put it—was their transcending loyalty. As early as 1759 an English parson named Andrew Burnaby had shrewdly taken the measure of the rulers of the Old Domin-ion. He noted that the public character of the Virginians cor-responded with their private one: "they are haughty and jeal-ous of their liberties, impatient of restraint, and can scarcely bear the thought of being controuled by any superior power. *Many of them consider the colonies as independent states, unconnected with Great Britain,** otherwise than by having the same common king, and being bound to her with natural affection." This is precisely the position taken by Thomas Jefferson in 1774 in his famous *Summary View*. Sentiments like these are redolent of the American soil. Here we have a native growth; there is nothing English in it.

Local Officeholding. The first gentlemen of Virginia were, in reality, a working aristocracy. As we have seen they had to be experts in agriculture, know something of elementary manufacturing, display business talents, and act in many ex-ecutive capacities. To the community they owed, in addition, a political obligation. This at the very least implied service on the parish vestry.

The vestry had been brought into existence in connection with the establishment of the Church of England as the state church, and was designed to serve as the lay body whose duty it was to look after the ecclesiastical affairs of the local area called the parish. In each parish this body was made up of twelve of "the best Gentlemen of the Country." Until 1676

* The italics are mine.

the vestrymen and church wardens had been elected, but thereafter the vestries filled their own vacancies and became exclusive bodies. The principal church duties of the vestrymen were erecting and maintaining the church building and the chapels of ease in the parish, handling funds, and engaging the minister.

But it was in its political and social, rather than its ecclesiastical capacity, that the parish achieved its greatest importance. As the smallest unit of government in Virginia, it came closest to the everyday life of the people. The vestry publicly published all laws pertaining to servants, slaves, morals, and vital statistics; it posted notices about lost property, stray animals, runaway servants, and the docking of entails; it announced all the governor's proclamations. Of first importance to everyone was the power of the vestry to apportion among the freeholders their shares of the tithes, or taxes, for the support of the church as well as the county and colony levies. The care of the parish poor also devolved upon this body of gentlemen, who were authorized to lay taxes for their support. Often, also, where no county or provincial authority interposed, vestries assumed the initiative for erecting ferries, opening roads, and founding schools.

To the planter, fresh from unchallenged authority over his own little patriarchal domain, the occasional meeting of the vestry served as the vital second step of his political training. Here he sat with eleven other planters who were his equals and determined what was best for the middling and inferior folk of the parish. Membership in vestries had become virtually hereditary by 1750, and collectively the vestrymen made up a sort of panel from which Virginia's rulers were drawn. Government was their business quite as much as the raising of tobacco because their birth, place, wealth, education, practical training, and frequently intelligence, fitted them to rule.

Membership on a vestry board was a local honor highly prized, and its meetings were unusually well attended. During George Washington's years of service as a vestryman of Truro Parish, 1763-1774, thirty-one meetings were held. He missed only eight, and these for such valid reasons as sickness, attendance at the House of Burgesses, and absence from the county.

Like the management of a great plantation, membership on the vestry was regarded as a prerogative of the aristocracy. Here in Virginia's smallest unit of local government, public servants were self-appointed and, with the passage of years, increasingly tended to act independently of the people. The average Virginian knew at first hand about taxation without representation because of his annual experience with the local vestry. On the other hand, vestries generally performed their duties to the parish faithfully, though hardly efficiently, and always of course, without charge. Whatever its weaknesses, and there were many, the parish vestry became the great nursery for Virginia's statesmen.

The only other governmental unit of which the majority of Virginians of the eighteenth century were aware was the county. Here again the people were witnesses to rule by the rich, the well born, and the *responsible* few. The royal governor at Williamsburg was authorized by law to appoint eight justices of the peace in each county, though in 1769 their numbers ranged from seven to twenty-four per county. Only members of the upper class ever received these coveted appointments to membership in the squirearchy, which, as in England, symbolized social recognition and opened the way to political preferment. When a vacancy occurred in any county, the justices submitted three names from which the governor made his choice. Thus, like the vestry, the county justices tended to become a self-perpetuating group.

If a Virginia justice of the peace took his duties seriously, as was often the case, he paid heavily for the honor, because the office was both burdensome and time-consuming. Acting as a local magistrate he heard both civil and criminal small causes. From his decision an appeal might be taken to all the justices sitting as a full bench at the county court. Each month, on a day specified by law, four or more justices met regularly at the county courthouse to record deeds and probate wills, to hear civil suits to the value of twenty-five shillings or two hundred pounds of tobacco, and to try criminal cases not involving the death penalty.

Court day was a gala occasion, and the sessions were always well attended because Virginians liked few things better than a lawsuit. At Leesburg, seat of Loudoun County, in December, 1774, Nicholas Cresswell listened to "a great number of litigious suits. The people seem to be fond of Law. Nothing uncommon for them to bring suit against a person for a Book debt and trade with him on an open account at the same time. To be arrested for debt is no scandal here."

Surpassing judicial duties in importance, however, were the executive and administrative burdens saddled on the county officials by the Assembly, which passed laws and cavalierly left their administration to local authority. The court made up the list of titheables, apportioned and collected the colony's taxes as well as the taxes for county activities. Opening and maintaining highways, erecting bridges, superintending ferries, regulating tobacco warehouses, licensing taverns, and conducting elections all came within the purview of the justices.

Often, too, where provincial legislation was lacking, the court passed ordinances governing runaway servants or slaves and other local matters.

Frequently, as one would expect, county officials were snowed under by this avalanche of duties. Viewed from almost any angle the Virginia system of county government appeared inefficient. The justices were amateurs, more often than not ignorant of law and government and devoid of any inclination to read up on it. Since they were unpaid, their sole incentives were honor and the public service. Many, like Richard Bland, Edmund Pendleton, George Mason, and Richard Henry Lee, worked hard at their jobs; others proved mere time-servers, often lazy and incompetent, who, being appointed for life, unfortunately could not be removed.

Cumbersome and inept as the county court came to be, this institution was, nevertheless, well suited to the temper and to the grievances of the people of Virginia. Justice was rendered on a person-to-person basis. Decisions were governed by the unwritten custom of the community which guaranteed the citizen protection against the routine tyranny of the modern judicial system wherein the observance of the letter of the law not infrequently throttles the spirit that gives it life. Everyone who could attended at the courthouse when the justices convened. Business and sociability competed with the rendering of justice on such occasions. Sooner or later virtually every freeholder came to know who the judges were and to have a pretty good idea whom he desired among the gentry to represent him as a burgess at Williamsburg.

Notwithstanding the rural isolation in which they lived, Virginia freeholders, or small property owners, were politically alert, and they would travel great distances to exercise the franchise. After 1762 anyone possessing twenty-five acres and a house, or fifty acres of uncleared land, could vote in the election of burgesses. It is not generally realized that the right to vote was not only as widely conferred in Virginia as in the Middle and New England colonies, but it was more widely exercised. In Virginia elections one white in eleven took part as compared with one in fifty in Massachusetts. Of course it must be noted that Virginians had no vote or voice in local matters at all, whereas the New England town meeting provided a great forum for the political training of the average man.

The primary political and social fact of eighteenth-century Virginia was rule by a class. The gentlemen of Virginia believed implicitly in the right of their class to rule; the proper business of the gentry was politics. Election laws stated that freeholders should choose "the best men of the country"; and custom decreed that only members of the upper class were selected. True, the gentlemen vied with each other for freeholders' votes, and, in defiance of the law, treating with liquor before the sheriff opened the polls was so common a practice that Colonel Robert Munford, burgess from 1765 to 1775, openly scored the abuse in a three-act satire of a county election called *The Candidates*, written in the early seventies. In 1774 at Alexandria, when Colonel George Washington and Major Charles Broadwater were elected burgesses, they "gave the populace a Hogshead of Toddy . . . [and] In the evening the returned Member [Mr. Washington] gave a Ball to the Freeholders and Gentlemen of the town." Aristocrats who, like Robert Wormeley Carter and James Madison, "never ask'd but one man to vote" for them, generally failed of election. Even "the best gentlemen," it appears, had to "familiarize" themselves "among the People" by the "corrupting influence of spirituous liquors, and other treats having a like tendency," since to the voters there were gentlemen and gentlemen.

In theory, power in colonial Virginia proceeded from the top downward—from the king to the governor to the Assembly to the county and ultimately to the parish. By the time it seeped through these several layers of authority and acted upon the individual it was pretty thoroughly diluted. Viewed from the bottom upward, it is clear that the parish and the county enjoyed virtual autonomy. Only once a year, when taxes and quit rents on land were collected or occasionally at election times and at militia musters, did Virginians become aware, even, of the government at Williamsburg. Whether in the Tidewater or in the Piedmont, they all lived in the country. To them government was largely an abstraction, except the county court and the vestry where the rule of gentlemen whom they knew by name was personal and easygoing. Local aristocrats usually were "the best people," and their trusteeship was accepted and approved by the lower classes who were entirely willing to leave colony matters to their betters. What went on in London was upon the whole a matter of indifference to them, though to the gentry it was a vital matter, especially if it impinged on their political status.

A striking instance of the ready assent of the common people of Virginia to rule by the first gentlemen and their confidence in this leadership occurred in 1774 when Benjamin Harrison was setting out to represent his colony at the First Continental Congress. A number of "respectable, but uninformed inhabitants" of the neighborhood waited upon him, and their spokesman said: "You assert that there is a fixed intention to invade our rights and privileges; we own that we do not see this clearly, but since you assure us that it is so, we believe the fact. We are about to take a very dangerous step, but we confide in you, and are ready to support you in every measure you shall think proper to adopt."

By the time a gentleman of the Tidewater came to be elected to represent his county in the House of Burgesses at Williamsburg, he had been exposed to an unsurpassed opportunity to school himself in what might be called the art and mystery of governing people. Commencing with control over his personal servant as a little boy, he gradually assumed more and more authority on the plantation; at maturity he took his "hereditary" seat on the parish vestry; soon thereafter he advanced to the office of justice of the peace. Many youthful planters held these offices in their early twenties and, on the thresholds of their careers, acquired at first hand a priceless apprenticeship in executive, administrative, and judicial work. If they were serious and curious like Robert Carter, Thomas Jefferson, and others, they employed the leisure time afforded by plantation life in supplementing their practical experience with the study of history and public law. Intellectual exercise never attracted the bulk of the gentry, but to the cream of the ruling class, to its thinkers and leaders, it appealed mightily. They became the great statesmen of the Old Dominion. Ideals of self-government and home rule were inculcated in these Virginians by the actual facts of their existence, while in their libraries they found the historical precedents for their position and worked out a theory on which they could base their course of action if their position should ever be threatened.

3

THE ROAD TO WILLIAMSBURG

A minute examination of one small segment of history frequently provides a clearer understanding of its meaning than
an attempt to chronicle the whole. For this reason the year
1765, which was decisive for the Old Dominion, has been
singled out as the best for study of the Virginia political mind
in action. It was in that year that members of the House of
Burgesses placed the Old Dominion in the van of colonial opposition to the new imperial policy of the Crown. If we
would know how this came about we can do no better than
join two imaginary planters and share vicariously with them
the adventures and excitement of that year; although these
men are fictitious, the scenes they viewed and the events they
participated in are real.

All roads leading into Williamsburg began at a plantation.
From one in the Northern Neck, as the area between the
Potomac and Rappahannock rivers was called, the two gentle-
men set forth on horseback on April 24, 1765 on a journey to
Williamsburg where they would represent their county in the
House of Burgesses. Only a combined sense of obligation to

the public and a desire to reap the prestige of membership in the House of Burgesses could have impelled them to exchange the conveniences and pleasures of their estates for the uncomfortable and tedious ride of 120 miles to the distant capital.

The numerous rivers and creeks of the Old Dominion cut deeply into the country, and consequently the great north-south post road ran inland at the head of navigation of these streams to make ferrying easier. Even so the crossings were costly. Perhaps the largest expense a county had to bear in any one year was the item of ten shillings per day plus ferriage for each of its burgesses who attended the sessions of the Assembly.

As they rode along from King George Court House on the way to the Rappahannock, the elder of the two travelers, who had sat in the Assembly for more than ten years, pointed out places of special interest and explained to his youthful and newly-elected companion the several matters of political business that would probably come up at this session. There were rumors about the accounts of Speaker John Robinson, Treasurer of the Colony; Mr. Lee of Westmoreland had hinted that Mr. Robinson's friends were being favored in a manner incompatible with sound public policy. Then there would be the tax bill and the matter of the Cherokee Indians ruthlessly killed in Augusta County by some whites. But more important than all of these was the question of whether or not Parliament had passed the odious stamp taxes, against which both Council and Burgesses had protested so warmly last December when the Assembly had been "in a flame" over the matter.

Reaching Port Conway they ferried across the Rappahannock to Port Royal, a tiny village boasting several tobacco warehouses, a wharf, and a few stores wherein Scottish merchants catered to the needs of nearby plantations. The tavern, or ordinary as Virginians usually called it, at the ferry was a sorry place with poor accommodations, but since it was all the town afforded, the gentlemen from the Northern Neck were forced to bait their horses and spend the night there.

On the twenty-fifth they rode leisurely across Caroline County, a region heavily wooded with only an occasional clearing containing a rude, unpainted, frame dwelling and its dependent buildings. The younger burgess remarked that despite the illiteracy and ignorance of the "commonalty and farmers" they encountered, their fields showed greater "marks of fine husbandry and improvement" than some he had seen in a recent journey to New England, though he added that they were not to be compared with those of the province of Pennsylvania. Both men, however, accustomed as they were to bountiful plantation meals, could scarcely stomach the luncheon of salt pork, dried fish, and hominy, which seemed to be the staple diet not only of the farm where they had stopped but of the average yeoman family throughout Virginia.

As the two riders reached the junction of their road with the King's Highway just outside Bowling Green, they were overtaken by a carriage drawn by six spirited horses, which rolled past them stirring up a great cloud of dust. When they dismounted at Roy's Tavern some minutes afterward they saw the carriage in the yard and learned from the Negro groom that it had come from Cleve on the Rappahannock and that its passengers were Colonel John Tayloe of the Council of State and Burgess Landon Carter, masters respectively of Mount Airy and Sabine Hall in Richmond County —two of the most imposing plantation houses in the Old Dominion. When the younger burgess expressed surprise that two such elegant gentlemen should condescend to stop over-night at a village ordinary, his companion informed him that their host was a man of family.

Before dark other gentlemen in periwigs traveling to Wil-liamsburg arrived at this genteel hostelry, and soon its public rooms resounded with excited discussions about tobacco, horses, cockfights, and stamp taxes, and with the rattling of dice boxes.

Arising early on the twenty-sixth, the travelers got a long start on their bibulous companions of the previous night. Leav-ing Bowling Green they followed the road which turned sharply to the east, passed Caroline Court House, and came into the beautiful plantation country lying between the Rappahan-nock and the Mattaponi, where the seats of many prominent planters were located. Riding along an excellent level road, they went through heavily wooded tracts broken occasionally by open fields. "If you really wish to see the great houses," re-marked the elder man, "you must travel by the rivers."

Spring was well advanced; the air was balmy and invigorat-ing, and the green haze of newly opened leaves formed a deli-cate background for the dogwood and other flowering trees. Although the day was unseasonably warm, the scanty cloth-ing of the slaves toiling in the tobacco fields excited the atten-tion of the younger burgess, and he observed too, that as in the Northern Neck, "Tobacco swallows up all Things, every-thing else is neglected." His friend told him that when he re-turned this way in June he would probably see many more Negroes in the clearing and "the greater part without any clothing."

They reached Todd's Bridge in King and Queen County by mid-afternoon, and though there was yet ample time to push on to King William Court House, they decided to tarry at William Todd's neat and comfortable tavern because several gentlemen at Roy's had reported the King William ordinary to be "disorderly and ill-kept." On a hill overlooking the Mattaponi was "The Mount," residence of Mr. Todd, and down by the bridge he had thrown across the river were his ordinary, warehouse, and wharf where several vessels were loading tobacco. The small settlement springing up here at the head of navigation on the river was typical of many to be found on Virginia's other streams at this time.

The next morning the travelers crossed Todd's Bridge and followed the road to King William Court House, where they turned south, and after a ride of twenty-five miles, came to the Pamunkey River. As they rode to Williams' Ferry, they could see on the New Kent bank the mansion house at Poplar Grove where their friend Richard Chamberlayne resided. They were delayed some time at the ferry, which was bringing the northern post rider across, but were rewarded for their patience by the loan of the latest copy of the *Virginia Gazette* from the ferry keeper. Crossing safely at last, they received a royal welcome from the master of Poplar Grove who regaled them after supper with the tale of Colonel George Washington's first meeting with Martha Dandridge Custis at Poplar Grove when on a journey similar to theirs in 1758.

The following day was spent agreeably in viewing several nearby plantations, including a visit to Colonel Burwell Bassett at Eltham, and in the evening they rode over to the ordinary at New Kent Court House, where they found good accommodations for both men and horses.

On the next morning an incident occurred about two miles

WHERE THE VESTRY MET
St. Peter's Church, New Kent County

THE SCENE OF COURT DAYS

*Hanover County Courthouse, where Patrick Henry made his
first great oration*

A SMALL PLANTER'S DWELLING

The Glebe (Houchin's Place), King William County

THE ORDINARY AT NEW KENT COURT HOUSE

*Since the two travelers stopped here in the eighteenth century, a
second story has been added to the structure, one of the few
remaining old taverns in Virginia*

A POOR PLANTER'S HABITATION

*In such a place as Liberty Hall in New Kent County the Jarratt
family lived*

JAMES CITY COUNTY COURTHOUSE, WILLIAMSBURG

Erected in 1770, this structure stands on the opposite side of the square from the building the travelers saw in 1765

from the courthouse, which doubtless meant little to two gentlemen such as they but which speaks volumes to us today, revealing as nothing else can the well-nigh insuperable barriers that existed in the eighteenth century between different classes of white people.

As the burgesses came upon a clearing, a group of children playing in a dooryard, suddenly seeing the horsemen with their fine clothes and wigs, turned and scampered off as fast as they could. These youngsters belonged to an industrious middle-class family of English and Irish descent who owned 1,200 acres of mediocre land but no slaves. The Jarratts were highly respected in the neighborhood, and one of the little boys, Devereux, who in later years became a famous Episcopal minister, recalled his impressions of the people "who lived beyond" his "humble station" and drank tea and coffee. "I suppose the richer sort might make use of those and other luxuries, but to such people I had no access. We were accustomed to look upon what we called gentle folks, as beings of a superior order. For my part I was quite shy of them, and kept off at a humble distance. A periwig, in those days, was a distinguishing badge of gentle folk—and when I saw a man riding the road, near our house, with a wig on, it would so alarm my fears, that, I dare say, I would run off, as for my life. Such ideas of the difference between gentle and simple, were, I believe, universal among all of my rank and age." Social inequalities were regarded as normal; every class accepted what Daniel Defoe had called "The Great law of subordination."

After eating an indifferent midday meal at Doncastle's in James City County, the travelers rode on and put up for the night ten miles from Williamsburg at Chiswell's much-frequented ordinary (the present Toano), where gaming with cards and dice went on into the small hours. Indulgence in such pursuits was responsible for a late start in the morning. It was high noon as the gentlemen from the Northern Neck reached the goal of their six days' journey, and, passing the three brick buildings of the College of William and Mary on their right, turned into Duke of Gloucester Street. Reining in their horses they gazed down the mile-long vista to the Capitol from whose flagstaff proudly waved the Grand Union of Britain. This was Williamsburg, seat of the empire of Virginia.

As they rode slowly down Duke of Gloucester Street, the deep sand and dust muffling the sound of the horses' hoofs, it was apparent that the end of the town near the college was largely residential. Most of the places of interest were on the north side of the street. After passing the yard and church of Bruton Parish, they halted to stare at the stately residence of Governor Fauquier at the north end of the Palace Green, and the veteran burgess pointed out on the west side the homes of George Wythe, Esq., and Councilor Robert Carter, two of the few large town houses that the village boasted; across the green stood the town hall, a wooden structure which had originally been built as a theater in 1716, the first in His Majesty's colonies.

Resuming their route "down town" they came to Market Square, a large open space on either side of the street, and noted on the right the courthouse of James City County in the distance behind a large brick magazine where the colony's powder was stored. Next on their left was a handsome brick house which belonged to the Ludwell's and was said to be one of the oldest in Williamsburg. A few doors farther on they dismounted at the Post Office to inquire for possible letters. Postmaster Joseph Royle also edited and printed the *Virginia Gazette* and conducted a stationery and bookstore in his little establishment. For future leisure reading, the men purchased several pamphlets about the stamp taxes, including *The Rights of the Colonies Examined* by Governor Stephen Hopkins of Rhode Island, and the two replies to it by Martin Howard, the Loyalist, in the letters of "A Gentleman from Halifax," as well as a copy of the newspaper just off the press.

The remainder of the way from the Post Office to the Capitol was lined with inns, ordinaries, and taverns, all alive with Negro servants running to and fro to accommodate the many travelers arriving for "Publick Times." On the right-hand side of the street they admired the elaborate signs of Wetherburn's noted house, the more exclusive Charlton's Inn, and the King's Arms. On the opposite side one came first to the Raleigh Tavern, a fine inn soon to rank with Philadelphia's City Tavern, the Green Dragon of Boston, and Fraunces' at New York as one of the most famous of revolutionary meeting places, and beyond stood other less expensive and more sedate establishments.

At the end of the thoroughfare they turned right on Blair Street for a few yards, then left down a path leading by the new Capitol (the first having burned in 1747) to the open area known as the Exchange, which was thronged at this time of day with gentlemen-planters, lawyers, merchants, ship captains, and peddlers settling accounts and transacting a multitude of business. Straight ahead on the east side of Waller Street they had a good view of the commodious new theater where Mr. Lewis Hallam held the performances of his American Company of Comedians.

Continuing to the end of Waller Street they turned left into York Road and rode a short distance to their lodgings at Mrs. Vobe's tavern. This attractive house was well situated, being near the Capitol, the Theater, the Coffee House, and the Race Track, and yet secluded enough to be quiet—at least, so one thought. After extensive and repeated instructions to the black hostler about the care and feeding of their horses, the two travel-stained men followed another slave boy, who carried their saddlebags, into the public room, where they were cordially greeted by Madam Jane Vobe and shown to their quarters.

"All the best people resorted" to Mrs. Vobe's, and the gentlemen from the Northern Neck soon learned that Sir Peyton Skipwith, William Byrd III and his kinsman Captain Le Foret of Barbados, Captain William Russell of the Fairfax militia, and Andrew Sprowle, a prominent Norfolk merchant, were staying there. Then, in addition, there was a droll Frenchman who told them in good English that all the guests of the tavern were professed gamesters, especially Colonel Byrd "who is never happy but when he has the box and Dices in his hand." "There were," he admitted, "many sets made at me to get me in for the box, but I had the good luck to Keep Clear of it, but Could not avoid playing some rubers at whist notwithstanding my aversion to it." This sad-faced Gallic complained that every public house in Williamsburg, including the excellent Mrs. Vobe's, was each night the scene of "Carousing and Drinking In one Chamber and box and dice in the other, which Continues till morning Commonly."

4

THE COLONIAL CAPITAL

In 1699 when the colony was nearly a hundred years old, Williamsburg was founded at Middle Plantation. Although the College of William and Mary had been opened there a few years previously, the town owed its eight decades of prosperity to the fact that it was the seat of provincial government. To this fact also it owed its social and economic importance and its significance as a focus of culture. When the capital was shifted to Richmond in 1780 the little community lapsed quietly into a state of somnolence and decay.

Most of the year Williamsburg was a sleepy little village, quite rural in appearance. There were about fifteen hundred people, white and black, and the houses, some 230 in number, were for the most part small, white, story-and-a-half structures—"every one detached from the other"—with little gardens of box, lovely flowers, and fruit trees. It possessed a singular charm of its own, resembling nothing so much, said Lord Adam Gordon, as "a good Country Town in England." It was chiefly a center for the plantations of the surrounding region and was much larger and more elaborate than the settlements around the courthouses or the river towns of Virginia.

The village did not play any great commercial role in the tobacco economy despite the residence there of several merchants, nor did it serve, like Fredericksburg and Richmond, as a distributing center for the back country. Still less was it a seaport like York Town or Norfolk. Markets were held twice a week; in April and December there were fairs; a few retail shops met the needs of town and country. Although numerous artisans practiced their crafts, the vogue in Virginia for things English condemned them largely to repair work, and Williamsburg developed no great native cabinetmakers like the Townsends and Goddards of Newport, or silversmiths comparable to Paul Revere of Boston or Joseph Richardson of Philadelphia.

On the other hand, certain continuing activities connected with the colonial government differentiated the capital from other Virginia communities. The presence of the royal governor and half a dozen members of the gentry insured the maintenance of a sort of provincial court and some off-season social life. Musical and scientific enterprises found sponsors in the governor and the college. Of incalculable cultural influence, as well as political and economic, were the newspapers published in Williamsburg. In 1755 William Hunter's *Virginia Gazette* asserted that the newspaper provides the people with "security against Errors, . . . no false doctrine in Religion, Policy or Physic, can be broached, and remain long undetected. . . . It is their great Preservation against political Empericism."

So decentralized was the colony's administration that there was relatively little work to be carried on in Williamsburg. Most of the business was in the hands of clerks in the secretary's office where reposed the great seal of Virginia. There, also, most of the colonial records were deposited; there vital statistics were kept; there one procured passes to leave the country. For most men, however, this office was important because it issued all land patents—the principal source of wealth in Virginia—in the form of fifty-acre grants to yeoman farmers or of huge tracts of thousands of acres to gentlemen with good connections and influence.

To the residents of Williamsburg, their own local concerns bulked much larger than those of the colony. They early felt the need for some kind of responsible government separate from York and James City counties, in each of which part of their town was located. The task was too great for the vestry of Bruton Parish. In 1722 Williamsburg received a royal charter incorporating it as a municipality with a mayor, recorder, aldermen, and common council to manage its affairs. Like vestrymen, these local officials constituted a self-perpetuating corporation, filling their own vacancies as well as designating the member of the House of Burgesses provided for Williamsburg by the charter. The mayor and aldermen sat monthly in a Court of Hustings and, since they concluded their business with considerable dispatch, merchants and others came to prefer to have suits decided there rather than in the lumbering county courts of York and James City. Meeting together in the "Common Hall" on the Palace Green, the mayor, aldermen, and councilmen were responsible for the welfare of the community—regulation of markets and fairs, licensing of taverns, supervision of buildings and roads, and, as a result of constant pressure from the *Virginia Gazette*, the establishment of a watch in 1772. Care of the poor was left in the hands of the parish vestry.

Because it was governed by a municipal corporation, Williamsburg was legally entitled to call itself a city. Such a designation is misleading, however, because of its modern connotation. Today the word *city* connotes size and urban congestion and suggests everything opposite to the word *rural*. As we have seen, the real and the most attractive attributes of Williamsburg were—and still are—those of a rural community. As one of its finest citizens, St. George Tucker, said: "few villages can boast of a more pleasant situation, more respectable inhabitants, or a more agreeable and friendly society."

Thus did the capital of Virginia stand in marked contrast with those of other leading colonies—Charles Town, Newport, Boston, New York, and the metropolis of Philadelphia, commercial centers whose large populations, ranging from 12,000 to 40,000, and compact urban environments made them comparable in size and, indeed, in economic and cultural importance to many of the prominent cities in Europe.

Twice a year at "Publick Times," when the General Court met and also on those occasions, as in May, 1765 when the Assembly convened, Williamsburg was "crowded with the gentry of the country" and their hangers-on, and the population doubled. The onset of "Publick Times" effected a mighty transformation in the village. If any proof of the town's dependence on the government and the plantation country was needed, this was it. Society and trade followed politics. Courts, markets, and fairs opened; people arrived from all parts of the colony to look after their interests and transact affairs, or to see the show; sharpers came out of the ground and pickpockets showed up to relieve the unsuspecting of their money. And the love of horseflesh and gambling drew Virginians of

all ranks to the races; the track east of Waller Street was perhaps the most democratic spot in the Old Dominion.

The colorful activity and confusion on Duke of Gloucester
Street misled many observers into overestimating the number
of people in town for "Publick Times." Traffic was heavy.
Vehicles of every description—gaily painted imported car-
riages with liveried footmen, men astride blooded saddle horses
or nondescript nags, lumbering wagons, wheelbarrows—contested for primacy in the wide thoroughfare, while along its
"well kept sidewalks" coursed a throng of "strangers" and
townsfolk—finely gowned ladies escorted by silk-stockinged
gentlemen in great wigs, local artisans in leather aprons, yeoman farmers in long yarn caps, rollicking mariners, swagger-
ing hunters in buckskins from the back country, college boys,
an occasional garishly painted Cherokee, and always blacks of
every age, sex, and description. "I have been here three Days
and am heartily sick of it," declared the harassed Frenchman
on April 28, 1765: "In the Day time people hurrying back
and forwards from the Capitoll to the Taverns, and at night,
Carousing." He was careful to add, however, that "the Inhabitants are very Courteous and hospitable."

5

THE GREAT MACHINE OF GOVERNMENT

An impressive and dignified pageantry had attended the formal opening of the Virginia Assembly on Tuesday, October 30, 1764. Eleven gentlemen, clad in judicial robes, members of the Council of State for the Colony and Dominion of Virginia, assembled shortly after eleven o'clock in their chamber on the second floor of the Capitol, where they witnessed the administering of the oath to several new burgesses while awaiting the arrival of the Governor (for such the Lieutenant Governor was always called in Virginia).

Meanwhile, nearly everybody in Williamsburg gathered along Duke of Gloucester from the Palace Green to the Capitol to get a glimpse of the Governor as he passed by. At twenty minutes to twelve there was a rattle of arms as the guard came to attention, the Palace doors opened, and the Honorable Francis Fauquier, Esq., His Majesty's Lieutenant Governor and Commander-in-Chief of the Colony and Dominion of Virginia, came rapidly down the walk and entered his waiting coach. The footmen mounted to their places and

the Negro coachman drove his six spirited bays slowly down
the Green and along the Duke of Gloucester in order that the
cheering and gaping populace might have an opportunity to
see this proconsul who was about to open the Assembly with
all the pomp and splendor of the British Empire.

Alighting at the Capitol's gates, he bowed graciously to the
crowd and then briskly entered the building and mounted to
the second-floor lobby where a waiting lackey threw a
judge's robe over his fine suit of London-made velvet. Precisely at high noon, the doorkeeper announced the arrival of
the Governor, and the councilors stood at their places as President John Blair escorted him to his seat at the head of the
board.

As soon as the Council was seated the Clerk of the Assembly, Nathaniel Walthoe, was ordered to acquaint the Speaker
of the House of Burgesses, which was awaiting the summons
in its own hall, that "The Governor commands the immediate
Attendance of your House in the Council Chamber." Accordingly, Speaker John Robinson led the sixty burgesses across
the building into the Governor's presence where they ranged
themselves around the room and stood, the Council remaining
seated, while Fauquier "was pleased to deliver his speech." He
explained briefly that the Assembly had been called, "after a
long Recess . . . to go through the Business of the Country"
and enumerated divers particular "points for Deliberation."
At the end of the address, the Governor ordered the burgesses to return and choose a speaker, and he then immediately
left the Council Chamber and drove back to the Palace.

Each house thereupon set about preparing a "humble Address" thanking His Excellency for "his kind and affectionate
Speech." Through this traditional humility, however, glowed

the fierce aristocratic pride which led the councilors to assure him of "their cheerful concurrence in such measures as they shall judge conducive to the honor of the Crown and the Good of this Country," and the burgesses to state that "we persuade ourselves that we have so well convinced Mankind of our strict Attention to social Justice," that "we hope we shall always be excused when we decline any Measure (however proposed) that we do not think productive" of this end.

No such ceremony accompanied the opening of an adjourned session such as that of May 1, 1765. At eleven in the morning the House of Burgesses "met according to their Adjournment," continuing the meeting mentioned above which had broken up for Christmas. They proceeded immediately with its business, the first item of which was the examination of the credentials of the new members. In the speaker's chair sat John Robinson. Then there were Attorney General Peyton Randolph and his brother John; Edmund Pendleton and George Wythe, foremost lawyers of the Old Dominion. Present also were many great planters, Carter Braxton, Archibald Cary, Landon Carter, a brace of Lees, Robert Munford, and many more.

Gathered here in one room was the flower of Virginia's political talent. They were, taken as a whole, indeed the best men of the Old Dominion, and there is little doubt that their leaders could compare in quality with any assembly in British America.

The House of Burgesses was a tobacco planter's club, to which, ordinarily, only members of the gentry or those associated with them were elected. Here one class determined what was necessary and good for the country, or to use its own phrase, what constituted "social Justice." Among its members there was wide agreement on a considerable body of opinion; they differed principally over means, not ends. Not one of them ever doubted the competence, or, in recent years, the right of the Virginia Assembly to determine the internal affairs of the colony, and, what was more important, all of them regarded outsiders, including Parliament, as lacking either the knowledge or the authority to do so. Interference with the self-government they had enjoyed in fact for so many decades they would resist as well as resent. In 1759 a traveler had observed that these gentlemen regarded themselves as being on the same social plane as the British gentry and superior to them in virtue. From this assumption it followed that the representative bodies of coequal aristocracies must be coequal parliaments functioning under the same sovereign.

The House of Burgesses consciously and assiduously followed every precedent and mode of procedure of the House of Commons that was locally applicable, and took careful account of all developments in English parliamentary practice. With each new year came an increase in the dignity and the parliamentary wisdom of the House of Burgesses. By 1764 it had become a supremely able and self-reliant body.

Among these elected members of the aristocracy an easy familiarity obtained; genuine democracy existed in this assemblage of equals. The speaker and the clerks alone wore robes. Burgesses remained covered and dressed as they chose: the Williamsburg members in fine suits and silk stockings, those from a distance not infrequently in boots and riding clothes. It mattered not, though visitors were inclined to mistake the informality of the chamber for lack of dignity.

Any such belief was dispelled when one of the great speak-

ers arose and addressed the House. Today when adroitly managed committee work determines whether most bills will pass
or not, it is exceedingly difficult to comprehend the prime importance of oratory in the eighteenth century. The burgesses
were not harassed by the pressure of business like our modern
lawmakers; they had ample time for debate. Eighteenth-century legislators did not make speeches largely for the benefit
of their constituents in the manner of the present; they addressed themselves to their fellow members who were independent judges of the issues before the House. During these
years about two-thirds of the members attended each session,
thereby insuring a good audience for those who had something to say. Here a gentleman had the much coveted opportunity to excel in the presence of his peers, for oratory, like
the great houses, bore the seal of aristocratic approval. Long
speeches replete with classical allusions, elaborate imagery,
and glowing periods, that closed with sonorous perorations
delivered with measured phrase and gestures *actually did
change votes.* Critical John Adams, himself a great speaker,
was dazzled by the brilliant personnel of the First Continental
Congress, "every one of them an orator," and in this gentle
art of persuasion he rated the Virginians highest of all.

The House of Burgesses considered any injustice or any
grievance, no matter how petty, that Virginians chose to
voice. From each county the members brought petitions and
lists of complaints to Williamsburg where they were placed in
the hands of the important Committee on Propositions and
Grievances. The forty members of this Committee usually
met each morning immediately after nine o'clock prayers for
two hours of work before the House assembled at eleven.
There were other regular committees such as those for Privi-

leges and Elections, Public Claims, and Courts of Justice as well as committees for special purposes, but none of them attained the importance of their present-day counterparts.

The first half of the momentous session of 1765 was devoted to the consideration of petitions submitted by individuals praying for a special act, usually about land or the payment of a sum of money for services rendered or planned. The large number of private acts passed is surprising, but this legislation was normal, particularly when we recall that the Assembly represented a class which believed that what was good for it was also good for the country. The gentry's interests were naturally considered first, and once they were attended to the agenda was cleared for discussion and debate on the points alluded to in the Governor's speech and other matters of public concern.

Membership in the House of Burgesses was in no respect considered politically inferior to a seat in the upper house, which was known as the Council of State. Political power was the supreme goal of the aristocrat; it guaranteed the highest social prestige. Perhaps the most popular and certainly the most influential political figure in 1765 was John Robinson of King and Queen County who, since 1738, had been both Speaker of the House and Treasurer of the colony, the two offices being linked together. Conditions were already shaped in his favor when he became speaker, and being a man of the finest family connections with the strong backing of the vigorous Randolph clan, of amiable and generous instincts, winning personality and moderate abilities, Speaker Robinson became as popular as he was powerful. Over the years he built up a ruling clique based on family alliances which ran Virginia like a modern political machine. It could not be accidental that in the twenty-one assemblies that met between 1702 and 1775, King and Queen County received twelve chairmanships of committees, or that the most luscious political plums fell to relatives and connections of the Robinson-Randolph interest. Until 1760, the gentry as a whole seem to have acquiesced without complaint in this rule by a specially privileged segment of their group, although the exclusion of the Lees, so prominent in colony affairs prior to 1748, appeared rather pointed to some, including the Lees.

For Virginians the apex of the social and political pyramid was one of the twelve seats on the Council of State. The appointment was for life, conferred by royal grace and favor upon the recommendation of the governor. In theory, membership went only to persons of character and ability, but wealth and social station proved essential. In time the office tended to be restricted to scions of a few prominent families noted for their useful connections and conservative outlook. Preference was often given to gentlemen living in or near Williamsburg because it facilitated assembling at least five councilors necessary for a quorum at emergency meetings.

The councilors who met with Governor Fauquier in May, 1765 were John Blair of Williamsburg, who as senior member was president of the body and who was also Auditor General of the colony; Robert Carter Burwell of Isle of Wight; William Byrd of Charles City, third councilor of that name; Richard Corbin of King and Queen, Receiver General; Thomas Nelson, Secretary of the province, and his brother William from York; Peter Randolph of Henrico; Robert Carter of Nomini Hall in Westmoreland County; and Presley Thornton of Northumberland. Unlike the burgesses, the Council members were not restricted to one office as the enu-

Thomas L. Williams

THE RALEIGH TAVERN

From which was issued the call for the First Continental Congress

VIRGINIA'S CAPITOL: HERE GATHERED COUNCIL, COURT, AND BURGESSES

This painting by Howard Pyle shows the second capitol, which was built in 1752, five years after the first structure burned down. The present reconstructed capitol at Williamsburg was erected after plans for the first building

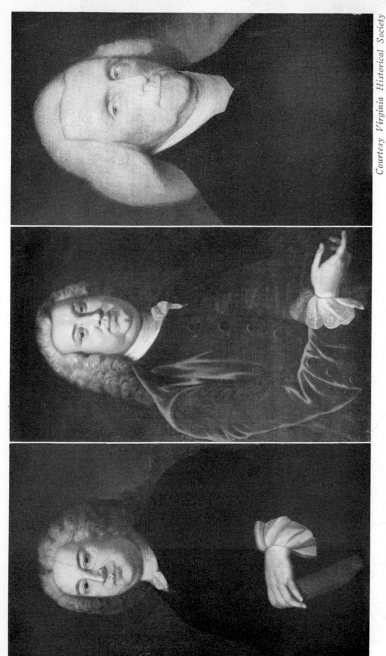

Speaker John Robinson   *Peyton Randolph*

Edmund Pendleton

BIGWIGS OF THE OLD DOMINION

FRANCIS FAUQUIER

Lieutenant Governor and Captain General of Virginia, 1758-1768

meration above indicates. In truth they monopolized all the important posts, and the income from the interest on funds they handled was considerable. But the greatest opportunity for personal aggrandizement came from the Council's control over land policy. Inequalities in land grants aroused discontent, especially in the Piedmont counties where many gentlemen resented the special privileges of this "independent oligarchy" almost as much as they did that of the Crown, but they were powerless to do anything about it.

In addition to the responsibilities of plural officeholding, a councilor had his regular duties which involved at least four different aspects of government. Each councilor was a colonel of the militia, which gave him a rank next to that of the governor. Then as the name suggested, the Council of State was expected to serve as an advisory board to the royal governor. It also constituted the upper house of the Assembly, and in this legislative capacity, tended increasingly to side with the burgesses against the governor, thereby vitiating its assigned role as a check on the lower house. Finally, with the governor, the members sat as judges in the General Court, the highest judicial body in the colony.

An Englishman visiting Williamsburg reported that "here the Courts of Justice are held, and with a Dignity and Decorum, that would become them even in Europe." Impressive though this General Court might appear, it proved to be the weakest branch of the Old Dominion's governmental system. The combination of chief executive and chief justice in the person of the governor did not escape comment. The other men who made up the court held positions of great trust and profit, and as members of the upper house, met in executive session and examined their own accounts, and at the same time sat in judgment on cases in which they themselves were interested. Such a procedure did not guarantee impartial justice. Josiah Quincy, Jr., an able Massachusetts lawyer, clearly perceived these defects, and very few of the local gentry were actually blind to them. That the councilors were gentlemen was not enough for some people.

The governorship was no mere hollow honor conferred on a royal favorite; it was an office of first importance. It is true that from 1705 to the arrival of Lord Botetourt in 1768, the titular governors of Virginia remained in England, but the appointee who actually came out to the colony held his commission directly from the king, and in the Old Dominion was always addressed and referred to as the governor. This commission gave him vice-regal powers as "Lieutenant Governor and Captain General." With the House of Burgesses and the Council of State he enacted all laws by giving his assent, and he enjoyed the all-important power to veto legislation. The governor was the chief executive of the province, with authority to make all major civil and military appointments as well as those to certain ecclesiastical offices. He could grant pardons. As captain general and vice admiral he commanded the military forces of the colony and could declare war or make treaties of peace. Then in his capacity as chancellor, he presided over the administration of justice in Virginia.

In theory, the royal governor, by virtue of his *commission* and a set of *instructions* issued in England, which in reality formed the constitution of Virginia, possessed not only the symbols but the substance of power. In fact, however, his position was unenviable. Royal authorities in England subjected his administration to constant review and frequently crippled his actions by issuing additional instructions that local conditions made impossible to enforce. In the seventeenth century the Council had pared down his authority; these "haughty Bashaws of the South" could make or break a governor. By 1750 the House of Burgesses, too, by applying a steady though quiet pressure, often abetted by the Council, had encroached on the prerogatives of the governor, actually the Crown's; and with each access of power, the confidence of the Assembly mounted. Thus it is clear that the royal governor had to serve two masters, the king and the Assembly of Virginia, and in endeavoring to please them both he often satisfied neither.

6

SOURCES OF CONFLICT

In Virginia politics of the mid-eighteenth century two features stand out prominently: the increasing resistance of the aristocratic ruling class, particularly through its House of Burgesses, to outside pressure and interference; and, down to 1765, the monopolizing of control within the Old Dominion by an entrenched coterie of the gentry headed by Speaker John Robinson. Examination of the course of events during these years will demonstrate better than anything else just what government by gentlemen was like, and also that the prevalence of steady habits is not always characterized by an absence of spirit. On several occasions there were indications that Virginians' definition of "loyalty" might eventually conflict with the interpretation of Englishmen at home, and in 1765 the issue was brought out into the open at Williamsburg. A decade later came revolution, war, and independence.

Back in 1748, after two years of constructive work, a committee of both houses of the Assembly completed a notable revision of the legal code which was well adapted to the needs of the province. Like all laws, these sixty-seven acts were sent

to London for the approval of King George II through his
Privy Council. Governor Dinwiddie announced on April 8,
1752, shortly after his arrival, that fifty-seven acts had been
allowed, but that ten had been disallowed because Governor
Gooch, Dinwiddie's predecessor, had disregarded his instructions providing that he should refuse to enact any law that
did not contain a clause suspending its operation until royal
approval could be obtained. Gooch had assented to the ten
acts because they were concerned with matters which could
not wait indefinitely for review.

This voiding of essential portions of the legal code revealed
in a dramatic fashion the extent to which a royal instruction
could deprive the Assembly of its initiative and even take
away its precious and hard-earned "right" of self-government.
Gone was the vaunted freedom of an earlier day. When an
"Address to the King" respectfully defending the disallowed
measures and urging reconsideration was rejected on the
grounds that the king's instructions must not be disregarded,
consternation spread over the colony, and as late as 1759 John
Mercer, eminent lawyer and burgess from Spotsylvania, told
the House "that it is a very difficult Matter to distinguish
which . . . Acts are in Force and which are not."

The year after the disallowance of the ten revised statutes,
the burgesses learned from the petitions of several of the western inhabitants of the Old Dominion that they were being re-
quired to pay for land patents a fee of a pistole (about four
dollars) more than under former governors. Promptly the
House addressed Governor Dinwiddie denying his right to
make this additional charge on the grounds that "the Rights
of the Subject are so secured by Law, that they cannot be deprived of the least Part of their Property, but by their own

Consent." Dinwiddie answered by dissolving the Assembly.

This foray of the burgesses uncovered the legal and literary talents of Richard Bland, who sat as a member from Prince George County from 1742 to 1775. A conservative among conservatives, Bland nevertheless brought the position of the lower house before the public in *A Fragment on the Pistole Fee, Claimed by the Governor of Virginia*, published at Williamsburg in 1753, wherein he graphically likened liberty and property to ships whose soundness is destroyed by springing the smallest leak in their seams. Today it seems that the Governor's fee was legal, if unwise, and that the argument advanced by the burgesses was somewhat specious, but the lasting historical significance of the dispute over the pistole fee lies in the determined and spirited stand of the members on the matter of taxation.

Soon the power of the Crown to veto colonial legislation again stirred up trouble. Every clergyman of the Church of England, by a law of long standing, received an annual salary of 16,000 pounds in tobacco. This amount was regarded as a fair money equivalent when the crop was normal. A drought in 1755 sent the price soaring, and, to give the planters some relief, the Assembly passed an act, probably drawn up by Richard Bland, permitting the payment of the clergy's salaries in money at the rate of twopence per pound of tobacco for the ensuing ten months. Because this was an emergency measure and its proponents felt that it was not feasible to wait a possible four years for review in London, the suspending clause was omitted. The clergy seized upon this omission and petitioned the Bishop of London to take up their cause with the royal authorities. Three years went by without a response from the Privy Council. In 1758 another drought resulted in a short tobacco crop, and upon petition from affected planters, the Assembly again passed a Two Penny Act allowing all taxes, debts, and fees to be paid in money at the same rate as before for the duration of one year. Governor Fauquier also gave his assent to this measure, which seems to have been framed by Mr. Bland.

Faced with a diminution of their incomes the clergy sent over the Reverend John Camm, Professor of Divinity at the College of William and Mary, to plead their case in London. Through his efforts, the Privy Council, four years after the first emergency act, issued an order on August 10, 1759 disallowing the laws, and Camm sailed home assured that the Privy Council's action rendered the measure void from the very beginning. In Virginia, therefore, several parsons brought suit to recover the difference between what they had been paid in money and the market value of 16,000 pounds of tobacco.

One does not have to take sides in the "Parson's Cause" to see that the fundamental issue was relief for the taxpayers, which was urgently needed, and that the relief had to come sooner than normal channels would permit. A public emergency existed. To the legislators the requirement of a suspending clause in an emergency measure had the precise effect of nullifying the measure, and it was therefore regarded as a constitutional practice interfering with the public welfare. Such obstruction was tyrannical as well as stupid. The burgesses appointed a committee consisting of Attorney General Peyton Randolph, Richard Bland, George Wythe, Robert Carter Nicholas, and Dudley Digges to defend their course. The committee instructed the agent in London to admit that the omission of the obnoxious clause was contrary to the royal will, but to argue that if the Crown's instructions were carried out in every case the colony's privilege of making its own laws would be greatly curtailed.

Now the best minds in Virginia concentrated on this great issue. Richard Henry Lee of Westmoreland argued the local case, not very convincingly it must be said, in a petition to the Crown which he planned to present to the Assembly for adoption. But it was Richard Bland, the Nestor of the House, who phrased the Virginia point of view in a language the people could understand. In 1760 William Hunter, printer, published *A Letter to the Clergy of Virginia* in which Bland forcefully contended that the public good is the highest law, and that the governor and the Council should constantly bear in mind that "where this Necessity prevails, every Consideration must give Place to it, and *even these Instructions may be deviated from with Impunity*."* Four years later this "very old experienced veteran . . . staunch and tough as a white-leather," who, as a friend observed, had about him "something of the look of musty old Parchme[n]ts w'ch he handleth and studieth much," issued a second pamphlet, *The Colonel Dismounted, or the Rector Vindicated*, wherein with "horse-play raillery," as Jefferson thought, he demolished the parsons and their cause.

Richard Bland's constitutional stand in *The Colonel Dismounted* represented an important advance from his previously published views and is of great significance in that it supplied the core of all later pre-revolutionary Virginia arguments. The colonists came here as English subjects in the seventeenth century, he says, and "under an English government all Men are born free, are subject only to Laws made with their own Consent, and cannot be deprived of the Bene-

* The italics are mine.

fit of these Laws without a Transgression of them." If, he continues, Virginians are born free and enjoy the rights of Englishmen, as they most certainly do, then they must have a legislature "composed in Part, of the Representatives of the people, who may enact laws for the INTERNAL Government of the Colony, and suitable to its various Circumstances and Occasions; and without such a Representative, I am bold enough to say, no Law can be made. . . . It is evident that the Legislature of the Colony have a Right to enact ANY law they shall think necessary for their INTERNAL Government."

The suit for the recovery of his salary brought by the Reverend James Maury in Hanover County in 1763 became one of the most celebrated law cases in American history. In November the court ruled that the parson was legally entitled to damages and, in December, instructed the jury to determine the amount. At this point the defense called in Patrick Henry, a young lawyer of the locality, to address the jury.

In this, his first important appearance before the public, Henry intuitively used a formula which he ever after found successful in swaying Virginia audiences. In the words of a modern writer, this was "to strive with terrific oratorical power after he had assured himself that he was in the wake, not the van, of a yet inarticulate public opinion." Fully aware that the taxpayers were against the clergy, whom he termed "rapacious harpies," and that the gentry had already expressed its resentment of the royal instruction requiring a suspending clause for each act, he unfolded and popularized, with moving eloquence and apparent boldness, Richard Bland's arguments. The Two Penny Act of 1758 was a good law, Henry insisted; the country needed it. Hence "a King by disallowing Acts of this salutary nature, from being the father of his people, degenerated into a Tyrant, and forfeits all right to his subjects' obedience." By the fiery delivery of a three-year-old argument which roused the people because it voiced their own sentiments and caused among some few present "a confused murmer of Treason, Treason," young Henry leaped at one bound into the center of the Virginia political ring. After the jury awarded damages of but one penny, Mr. Maury reported that Henry sought him out and apologized to him for what he had said, naïvely "alleging that his sole view in engaging in the cause, and in saying what he had, was to render himself popular."

This mounting opposition to the Crown and to its viceroy in Virginia, this steady assertion of legislative independence, this belief that a king who fails his people is a bad king and therefore a tyrant—all these were engineered and forwarded by the conservative Tidewater clique for whom Richard Bland was the spokesman. And in presenting such a spectacle, they were acting as aristocrats always have when kings fail to meet with their approval.

Within the gentry, however, there were many whose families were not in the inner circle, and who, though approving fully the stand of the House of Burgesses for self-government, began by 1759 at least to have an uneasy feeling that the select few were not conducting Virginia's affairs as they should. To them the true source of power was the great planter class, not the House of Burgesses: it was but the agency for expressing this power. Under the Robinson-Randolph administration there lurked the danger of aristocratic government degenerating into the self-seeking rule of an oligarchy. Some even feared that class would give way to caste. But just as aristocrats would turn against a bad king or the mob, so also would they, in time, discipline those of their own group who stepped out of line or monopolized privileges and favors that belonged to their class as a whole.

Another fact of which the inner clique took insufficient notice was the spread of their tobacco civilization beyond the Tidewater. In 1750 and succeeding years the Piedmont counties had ceased to be the wild frontier so condescendingly and pungently described by the second William Byrd thirty years before. Times had indeed changed. Below the head of navigation, or fall line, few new mansions were being erected; worn-out land had become the symbol of this area. Above the line, wealth was accumulating as this region became the center of tobacco culture as well as of population. There great houses like Prestwould, Castle Hill, and Rocky Mills were rising on the profits of slave labor as the percentage of the Piedmont's Negro population (45.4) almost equalled that of the Tidewater (49.4).

Land and slavery extended Virginia's aristocracy to the Piedmont counties. Scions of the older families came to sit on the vestries and county courts of the thirty-odd new counties represented in the House of Burgesses; Piedmont families freely intermarried with those of the Tidewater; they often came to represent more wealth; they ruled in their own counties; they reared young men of great political astuteness and ability. By the 1760's the center of gravity had shifted. This Young Virginia group, a western extension of the aristocratic Tidewater type, was ready to contest for a share in governing the Old Dominion with the Old Guard and, it should be added, for its share in offices and the other fruits of political power.

No greater mistake can be made than to regard the Pied-

mont gentlemen of 1765 as coming "from humble walks" of
life. Virginia's one baronet of that period, Sir Peyton Skipwith, lived at Prestwould in Mecklenburg County. Many burgesses from these upper counties had, without question, aristocratic family connections, as for example Dr. Thomas Walker
of Albemarle, Paul Carrington of Charlotte, John Fleming
and George Carrington of Cumberland, George Johnston of
Fairfax, James Littlepage and John Syme of Hanover, and
Robert Munford of Mecklenburg. No backwoods quality at-
tached to these men, nor did they savor of the yeoman middle
class. They were cultivated gentlemen, eager to exercise their
talents, and they resented the Tidewater monopoly of the best
offices. Possessing economic power in terms of land and slaves,
a developing culture, great energy, and an aristocratic pride
as sensitive as that of their eastern kin, they nursed their grievances until an opportunity should present itself. The balance
of the tobacco economy had tipped in favor of the gentlemen
of the upper counties and those who were foresighted realized
that sooner or later a comparable adjustment of the political
scales had to come. In the meantime, while they waited for an
issue, they eagerly scanned their ranks for a dynamic leader.

Yet so well entrenched were the Robinson-Randolph men
and so capable and popular was their leader that for a long
time both he and his followers were "elevated above the criti-
cism" of their faults. The two elements of potential opposition, the dissatisfied Tidewater families headed by the Lees
and the young aristocrats of the upper counties, were unable
to break through the crust of respectability and admiration
that protected the Speaker and his coterie.

Almost providentially, it now seems, the bungling ministers
of King George III presented Virginia's political "outs" with

their long-sought opportunity. In April, 1764 Parliament passed a series of resolves calling for duties on imports to the colonies and an increase in the tariffs on sugar and molasses, the proceeds of which were to be used for the support of British troops in America. It further declared that "it may be proper to charge certain Stamp duties" in the colonies.

Since the Assembly was not in session from January 1 to October 30 no official expression of Virginia opinion was offered. In May, however, Richard Henry Lee informed a London correspondent that the plans being made in England by George Grenville and the Ministry "seem to prove a resolution, to oppress North America with the iron hand of power, unrestrained by any sentiment, drawn from reason, the liberty of mankind, or the genius of their own government." He elaborated Bland's concepts of the "illegality of taxation without consent," and concluded prophetically that "possibly this step of the mother country, though intended to secure our dependence, may be subversive of this end."

The Assembly met on October 30 to listen to Governor Fauquier's speech which of course contained no mention of the proposed stamp taxes. The burgesses, however, were alarmed at the prospect before them, as were the leaders of their sister colonies, especially in New England, and, on the motion of Richard Henry Lee, appointed a committee including Peyton Randolph, George Wythe, and Lee to draw up representations against the measure to be sent to the Mother Country. Mr. Lee apparently desired to take as strong a position as that of his May letter to London, but Wythe and other conservatives restrained him. Commenting on these papers in their final form, Governor Fauquier reported to the Board of Trade that "I have been told by some Gentlemen of the

Committee appointed to draw them up, that their whole study has been to endeavor to mollify them, and they have reason to hope there is nothing now in them which will give the least offence." The difference of opinion over the nature of these protests probably explains the successive postponements of consideration of the subject from the time when the matter was first brought up on December 4 until December 14 when the House went into a Committee of the Whole with Peyton Randolph in the chair. If any incident can be said to mark the beginning of the revolt of Lee and his adherents from the authority of the "old members," it is this struggle within the Committee.

The Committee presented three documents for debate: an "Address" to "the King's Most Excellent Majesty" and a "Memorial" to the House of Lords, both written by Richard Henry Lee, and a "Remonstrance" to the House of Commons which the adroit conservatives arranged to come from the more restrained pen of the great jurist George Wythe. After several days of discussion, the three resolves, softened in tone by the burgesses in conference with the Council, passed both houses on December 18.

The gentlemen of Virginia, long accustomed to taking a high position where their "liberties" were concerned, had, in these state papers, merely refined for a British audience Richard Bland's doctrines of fifteen years earlier. They rehearsed the point that the colonists were "Britons," and that their rights as Englishmen had been confirmed by royal charters and over a century of usage. Their conclusion, stated more positively by Lee in the "Memorial" to the House of Lords than by Wythe in his "Remonstrance," was that Virginians "conceive it to be a fundamental Principle of the British Constitution, without which Freedom can no Where exist, that the People are not subject to any taxes but such as are laid on them by their own Consent, or by those who are legally appointed to represent them: Property must become too precarious for the Genius of a free People, which can be taken from them at the Will of others, who cannot know what Taxes such People can bear, or the easiest Mode of raising them; and who are not under that Restraint, which is the greatest Security against a burthensome Taxation, when the Representatives themselves must be affected by every Tax imposed on the People." Notwithstanding the efforts of some members "to mollify them," Governor Fauquier said of the resolves that "the terms are very warm and indecent." This at least was true, they were stronger than the addresses of any other colonial assembly except that of New York, and they defined the issue on which the opposition to the Stamp Act would ultimately focus—taxation without representation.

Colonial prayers and protests were made in vain; the Stamp Act became law on March 22, 1765 and was scheduled to go into effect on the first of the following November. This measure, requiring stamps paid for in sterling to be affixed to all legal documents, newspapers, pamphlets, almanacs, playing cards, and dice was an exercise of direct internal taxation which Virginians had always maintained was the exclusive right of their Assembly.

7

DIVISION AND REUNION

When the House of Burgesses met on May 1, 1765 news of the enactment of the Stamp Act had not reached Williamsburg, and the members proceeded to dispatch routine business: the issuing of a new writ for the election of a burgess from Louisa in the place of William Johnson who had resigned to become coroner of the county; the passing of many private acts; and an address to the governor requesting the offering of a reward for the detection of the "Assassins" of some Cherokee Indians in the Shenandoah Valley. Perhaps the most interesting event of the early part of this session was the debate on the case of Thomas Prosser, a member of the House from Cumberland County, against whom the Committee on Privileges and Elections brought charges on May 4 of "antedating, and advising, directing and assisting" in the alteration of certain deeds and conveyances; and also for forging a sheriff's name to a jury order by means of which he packed a jury and illegally secured a piece of land. Sitting in judgment on the qualifications of its member, the burgesses listened to a score of witnesses describe Prosser's overwhelming guilt; then

A PIEDMONT ESTATE IN MECKLENBURG COUNTY

Sir Peyton Skipwith's Prestwould

A PIEDMONT ESTATE IN ALBEMARLE COUNTY

Dr. Thomas Walker's mansion Castle Hill

Courtesy Am. Scenic & Historic Pres. Soc.   *Courtesy Virginia Historical Society*

Richard Henry Lee   *George Johnston*   *Patrick Henry*

HOT AND GIDDY MEMBERS

THE VIRGINIA STAMP ACT RESOLVES OF 1765

This contemporary copy of the resolves was once in the possession of Patrick Henry. It is now displayed in the reconstructed Capitol at Williamsburg, a gift of the heirs of Charles L. Hamilton of Philadelphia

THE
NEWPORT MERCURY.

Containing the freſheſt Advices, foreign and domeſtic.

MONDAY, JUNE 24, 1765.　　(Numb. 355.)

RHODE-ISLAND.

By ORDER of the HONORABLE
JOHN TEMPLE, Eſq;
Surveyor-General of His M——
Cuſtoms for the Norther——
of North-America.

WHEREAS the ——
Revenue requir——
Newport, be——
arriving in——
any othe——

Extract of a Letter from a Gentleman in Philadelphia, to
his Friend in this Town, dated laſt Tueſday.

" I HAVE incloſed the Reſolves of the Virginia Aſ-
" ſembly, on debating the Stamp Act. The Go-
" vernor, as ſoon as he heard what they were about, ſent
" for them, and without Preamble, told them, he would
" diſſolve them; and that Minute they were diſſolved.
" As they are of an extraordinary Nature, thought they
" might not be diſagreeable. They are as follows,"

" *WHEREAS* the Hon. Houſe of Commons, in England, have of late drawn into Queſtion, how
far the General Aſſembly of this Colony hath
Power to enact Laws for laying of Taxes and impoſing
Duties, payable by the People of this his Majeſty's moſt
antient Colony: For ſettling and aſcertaining of this
future Time; the Houſe of Burgeſſes of this preſent General
Aſſembly have come to the following Reſolves:

" *Reſolved,* That the firſt Adventurers, Settlers of this
his Majeſty's Colony and Dominion of Virginia, brought with
them and tranſmitted to their Poſterity, and all other his
Majeſty's Subjects ſince inhabiting in this his Majeſty's Colony
all the Privileges and Immunities that have at any Time been
held, enjoyed and poſſeſſed by the People of Great-Britain.

" *Reſolved,* That by two Royal Charters, granted by
King JAMES the Firſt, the Colonies and Immunities of this his
and entitled to all Privileges and Purpoſes, as if they thus
abiding and born within the Realm of England.

" *Reſolved,* That his Majeſty's liege People of this his
Subjects, have enjoyed the Right of being Taxes and
antient Colony have enjoyed the Right of being taxed
govern'd, by their own Aſſembly, in the Article of Taxes and
internal Police; and that the ſame have never been conſtantly recog-
nized by the King and People of Britain.

" *Reſolved,* That his Majeſty, or his Subſtitute,
or any other Way yielded up, but have never given up ſuch
this Colony, together with their Majeſty or his Subſtitute,
have, in their Repreſentative Capacity, the only excluſive
Right and Power to lay Taxes and Impoſts, upon the Inhabitants of this Colony: And that every Attempt to veſt ſuch
Power in any other Perſon or Perſons whatſoever, than the
General Aſſembly aforeſaid, is illegal, unconſtitutional and
unjuſt, and have a manifeſt Tendency to deſtroy Britiſh as
well as American Liberty.

" *Reſolved,* That his Majeſty's liege People, the Inhabitants of this Colony, are not bound to yield Obedience to any
Law or Ordinance whatever, deſigned to impoſe any Taxation whatſoever upon them, other than the Laws or Ordinances
of the General Aſſembly aforeſaid.

" *Reſolved,* That any Perſon, who ſhall, by ſpeaking or
writing, aſſert or maintain, that any Perſon or Perſons,
other than the General Aſſembly of this Colony, have any
Right or Power to impoſe or lay any Taxation on the People
here, ſhall be deemed an Enemy to this his Majeſty's Colony."

All ——
of Mr. ——
are deſire——
who have al——
hibit their ——

And to be S——

Joſeph Du——
At Store No ——
A great Varie——
conſiſting of B——
SUPERFINE Bro——
Serge Denim, Fla——
coloured Ducapes ; pie——
and black Mantuas ; b——
black corded Paduſoy, ſtri——
and pink coloured Perſians ——
and black Pelongs ; Mens——
black Sa in and buduſoy Rib——
blue, white and buff coloured ——
Sagathies, Iriſh Linens, Checks, ——
Cotton Hollands ; Mens and Wor——
and Worſted Hoſe ; Mens and W——
and coloured Gloves ; white and ——
Damaſk and Diaper Table Cloths, Calf——
Cotton and Wool Cards ; —good Aſſor——
Ware, Braſs Cocks, Knives and Fork——
Tongs, Hammers, Stock and Pad Loc——
and Weights, Pewter, Nails, Window——
Stone Ware ; a Parcel of neat Fowl——
hid Cordage, &c. &c.

Beſt Saltertuda Salt by the la——
ſmall Quantity, Sugar by the Barrel, choice P——
diſpo by the Dozen or ſingle P——d, Redwood, C——
wood, 10d. 8d. 6d. 4d. 2d. Nails, and a good ——
ment of Engliſh Goods to be ſold by Retale,

By *Job Bennet,* jun.

Who deſires all Perſons that are indebted to him——
Book, Note or Bond, which have not been adjuſted ——
above one Year paſt, to ſettle with him ſoon.

All Perſons indebted to the Eſtate
of JOSEPH COZZENS, late of Newport, deceaſed, are
deſired to make immediate Payment to us the Subſcri-
bers, Adminiſtrators of ſaid Eſtate : And thoſe who
have any Demands, are alſo deſired to bring them in,
that they may receive Satisfaction.

JOHN CASEY,
WILLIAM COZZENS.

Newport, 9th Third Month, 1765.
N. B. The Frame of a large Dwelling-Houſe, be-
longing to the Eſtate of ſaid Deceaſed, to be ſold by
the Adminiſtrators.

All Kinds of Spirits diſtilled and
SOLD BY

Frederick Hamilton,

At the lower End of the Town, by Wholeſale and Retale.

From —— ——kly CHRONICLE.
——NTER.

has lately ſtirred very
of ſuffering the colonies
entatives to the Bri-
attentively to the
ueſtion, and can-
ice and humanity
allow our ſettle
of the nation, if
eceſſary ſhare
ly eſtabliſhed
laves, nor en-
bjects to ſettle
to rob them
ives.
by the
eſield,
ws in
Eng-
er

I am very well aware that the advocates for arbitrary
power will make many objections againſt a propoſition
of this nature, as it is utterly repugnant to the views of
their employers. Ambitious men foreſee, that if the
number of repreſentatives is not encreaſed, the new ac-
quiſitions in America will in a few years enable them to
keep a conſiderable addition of voices in p y, both within
doors and without ; and put them in a mid-ſtate with a
capacity of tyrannizing over the kingdom, as if they
were rulers in the moſt arbitrary parts of the Eaſt, and
acting under the dictates of ſome rapacious *Subah* or
ſome blood thirſty *Mgul.* For theſe reaſons we muſt
expect to hear a variety of plauſible arguments againſt
the preſent propoſal, and no way wonder to find it treated, as dangerous, irrational, and abſurd. We ſhall be
told that ſuch a multitude of counſellors will create con-
fuſion ; but it is our buſineſs to recollect that they will
create ſafety alſo, and that no difficulties or inconveni-
encies are of conſequence enough to deter us from a
proper regard to our liberties and laws. Our glorious
anceſtors did not think death too great a price for the
preſervation of freedom ; and we ought not to think a
little trouble ſuch a hardſhip, where they parted ſo
liberally with their blood　　　　　　W. PYM.

VIENNA, March 23.

WE have an account from Carlſtadt, in Tranſyl-
vania, of a moſt ſhocking tranſaction which
paſſed at Carnor, about two leagues from that town.—
A man who had been a few months married to a young
woman of eighteen, of whom he was exceedingly jea-
lous, having taken ſome exceptions of her conduct,
locked himſelf up one evening with her and her mother ;
ſtripped his wife, and having faſtened her to the wall
wooden pegs, he cut off her ears, noſe, and two
and drove a ſtake into her belly. He then cut
ſide with a knife, and not finding her heart,
wanted, he opened the other ſide, from which
out. He then loosened the poor wretch,
the ground, to which he faſtened her with
after which he laid himſelf down by the
and as if being ſatiated with barbarity had
ſame effects with frunkenneſs, he fell into
ſeep, that his mother in law, who expected
opened the doors, and eſcaped unto
where ſhe gave an account of the
had been witneſs to. Proper per-
who feared this furious ſavage
the puniſhment inflicted on him
ſo unheard of a crime. The
manners of the antient Scythians,
to the gallows, where he
noſe, ears, and the fleſh of
hot pincers. He was to
out, but this was omitted,
becauſe a Catholic. They
ſall of his own horſe, and
und the gallows ; after
, one after the other,
they then cleaved his
out his heart, which
laſt his limbs were
dogs and wild animals
in fact devoured
ſeven torments
On the ſame
was taken up
from a lake

——regory Jar-
——ometime in

——the
——Ja-
——, ne-
highly admini-
exploits and pious
in all places, except
fluence of the unlimited autho-
——Puniſh. In this edict the Pope de-
——thoſe kingdoms, from whence the Jeſuits
——een expelled, or in which their order has been
——uppreſſed, are, and ſhall ever be, the objects of his de-
teſtation ; he charges them with calumny, and loads
them with invectives. The miniſtry have called the
Nuncio here before them to know what could reſtrain
his holineſs to publiſh ſuch an inſolent and ſcandalous
edict, and it is ſaid that this Papal Envoy has been forbidden to appear at court until this matter is properly
cleared up."

Courteſy Library of Congreſs

"AN ALARM BELL TO THE DISAFFECTED"

First publication of the Virginia Resolves in the Newport Mercury

they voted to expel him and to render him forever incapable
of membership in the lower house.

A few days later, a copy of the Stamp Act "crept into the
House," as the Governor put it. The members, despondent,
gave every indication of acquiescing; after all it was now a
law. It was nearing the end of the month; the business of the
burgesses slackened, and many of the Tidewater men, who
were "most averse to an absence from home," retired to their
plantations. Here at last were both the issue and the opportunity so long awaited by the nascent opposition.

Most political maneuvers are secretly arranged in confer-
ences, and the historian is consequently deprived of any written records from which he may reconstruct what took place.
Available evidence indicates that early in 1765 the Piedmont
members made a "deal" with some of the discontented Tidewater burgesses. Richard Henry Lee may even have absented
himself purposely from this session with the design of lulling
the Old Guard into security, for we know that he embraced
the new alliance with enthusiasm and brought several Tidewater members along with him. Among the managers for the
upper counties were John Fleming, "distinguished for his pa-
triotism and the strength of his mind"; George Johnston, "a
very able, logical and correct speaker"; Colonel Robert Munford, war veteran, county lieutenant, future poet and play-
wright; and Paul Carrington, jurist and intimate of Patrick
Henry.

Just what schemes they concocted may never be known.
They seem to have decided that Henry's uncanny sense of
timing which "made audacity safe," his popularity with the
freeholders, and his tremendous oratorical powers made him
the logical leader around whom they could successfully rally

their followers, and it is not too fanciful to suggest that they had a hand in his election to fill the seat from Louisa vacated by William Johnson. Certain it is that when Patrick Henry took his place in the House of Burgesses on May 20, 1765 and was immediately placed on the Committee for Courts of Justice, he had been designated one of the leaders of the western members, who were posted to stay until the end of the session. Henry knew this. He did not stand alone, or unmanaged, as he later stated. Politics does not work that way.

Meanwhile John Fleming was hard at work behind the scenes drawing up a set of resolutions, seven in number, intended as the answer of the House of Burgesses to the Stamp Act. Virginia was not going to submit without a protest. On May 23 Henry made his maiden speech in opposition to a plan fostered by Speaker Robinson to set up a public loan office to relieve the money shortage in the colony—and perhaps, also, some of his needy friends. Although the new member from Louisa, displaying a "bold, grand and overwhelming eloquence," attacked the scheme on general grounds, the measure passed the House only to be defeated in the Council where the Robinson forces were not so numerous.

Attendance continued to fall off until May 29 when the House was the "thinest ever known." The day began quietly enough with the approval of the treasurer's accounts and the reading and passage of several bills, including one to pay Peter Pelham £50 for repairing the organ at Bruton Church. After Archibald Cary reported a bill concerning the militia, the drowsy routine of the session came to an abrupt end as George Johnston of Fairfax rose and quietly moved "that the House resolve itself into a Committee of the whole House immediately to consider of the Steps necessary to be taken in Consequence of the Resolutions of the House of Commons of Great Britain relative to the charging certain Stamp Duties in the Colonies and Plantations of America." Mr. Henry seconded this motion, which galvanized the burgesses into tense activity.

When the House went into a Committee of the Whole, "Mr. Patrick Henry plucked the veil from the shrine of Parliamentary omnipotence" by offering, in succession, five of Mr. Fleming's resolutions against "the usurpations of parliament"! As he concluded his powerful advocacy of each one, George Johnston seconded it with a speech remarkable for "solid reasoning." In the course of the debates Paul Carrington and Colonel Munford were among the most eloquent supporters of the resolutions. This combination of fire and logic succeeded. Only thirty-nine members were present in the Committee of the Whole when the resolutions "were proposed and agreed too, all by very small majorities." Governor Fauquier reported to the Board of Trade: "I am informed the gentlemen [Henry, Johnston, and Fleming] had two more resolutions in their pocket, but finding the difficulty they had in carrying the 5th, which was by a single voice, and knowing them to be more virulent and inflammatory, they did not produce them." Well might they have refrained, for their "rash heat" was strenuously, and very nearly successfully, opposed by Speaker Robinson, Peyton Randolph, Richard Bland, and George Wythe.

The meager Journal of the House merely reports of the proceedings in the Committee that "after some Time spent therein Mr. Speaker resumed the Chair and Mr. Attorney [Peyton Randolph] reported the said Committee had had the . . . matter under their Consideration, and had come to several Resolutions thereon, which he was ready to deliver in at the

Table." It being late, consideration was put off until the next day.

The better part of the next morning was spent on a disputed election in Mecklenburg County and a bill to regulate the Indian trade. Then, much against his judgment and will, Attorney General Randolph rose in his place and, as Chairman of the Committee of the Whole, read the resolutions. Posterity is indeed fortunate that the observant Frenchman, whom we met earlier, has left an eye-witness account, written at the time, describing the beginning of the American Revolution in Williamsburg. Having arrived in town from York at noon, he records, "I went immediately to the Assembly which was seting, where I was entertained with very strong Debates Concerning Dutys that the parlement wants to lay on the American Colonys, which they Call or Stile stamp Dutys."

Few days in all of America's great and long legislative history have been so dramatic (or so misunderstood). The participants were supremely conscious of the importance of their action. All were patriotic Virginians; they differed not over principles. The resolutions merely restated in more vigorous language the views, and in places the very words, of the three papers sent to England by the Assembly in December. Why, then, did Bland, Randolph, and Wythe join Speaker Robinson to form a conservative phalanx to defeat endorsement of a paraphrase of their own ideas? The answer is that six months before when they uttered these sentiments it was safe to do so; now the Stamp Act was law, and danger lurked in defiance of Parliament. It would be better to take a more cautious course. Moreover each side knew that its stand for liberty also involved a struggle for political power, and each

tenaciously fought for its own cause in this great forensic bat-
tle—the one to seize the leadership, the other to retain it.

"Shortly after I came in," says the Frenchman, "one of the
members stood up and said he had read in former times tarquin
and Julus had their Brutus, Charles had his Cromwell, and he
Did not Doubt but some good american would stand up, in
favour of his Country, but (says he) in a more moderate manner, and was going to Continue, when the speaker of the house
rose and Said, he, the last that Stood up had spoke traison, and
was sorey to see that not one of the members of the house was
loyal Enough to stop him, before he had gone so far. Upon
which the Same member stood up again (his name is henery)
and said that if he had affronted the speaker, or the house, *he
was ready to ask pardon,** and he would shew his loyalty to
his majesty King G. the third, at the Expence of the last Drop
of his blood, but what he had said must be attributed to the
Interest of his Country's Dying liberty which he had at heart,
and the heat of passion might have lead [led] him to have said
something more than he intended, but, again, *if he said any
thing wrong, he beged the speaker's and the houses pardon.**
Some other Members stood up and backed him, on which that
afaire was droped."

It was not what Patrick Henry said, but rather the manner
in which he said it, that called forth Speaker Robinson's re-
buke. In the first flush of his triumph he had made the one
misstep of his whole oratorical career when, for an instant, he
forgot that although Virginians might be ready for treason-
able action, they, like many of their descendants, could not be
brought to relish the interpretation of such action in the language of sedition. "In his harangue," wrote Edmund Ran-

* The italics are mine.

dolph, some years later, Mr. Henry "certainly indulged in a strain never before heard in the Royal Capitol," and his "dexterous escape or retreat, if it did not savour of lively eloquence, was of itself a victory. . . . Not always grammatical, and sometimes coarse in his language, he taught [his hearers] how to forget his inaccuracies by his action, by varying countenance and voice. . . . He sounded the recesses and depths of the human heart."

Patrick Henry's oratory, sweeping reason before it, moved some members "classed on the other side of the controversy," and this, taken with the solid vote of those whom Fauquier contemptuously branded "the young hot and giddy members" from the upper counties, provided the slender margin of victory—"the greatest majority being 22 to 17; for the 5th Resolution, 20 to 19 only." In his old age, Thomas Jefferson recalled standing in the lobby of the House as Peyton Randolph strode out exclaiming, " 'by God I would have given 500 guineas for a single vote,' for one vote would have divided the House, and Robinson was in the chair, who he knew would have negatived the resolution." Leadership now moved beyond the fall line. This "the old members, whose influence in the house till then had been unbroken," bitterly realized.

Confident that he and his supporters had come triumphantly through the crisis he had so sensationally precipitated the day before, Patrick Henry mounted his "lean horse" and rode off to Hanover that evening, unaware of the tenacity and resourcefulness of the Tidewater gentlemen.

These are *the facts* of Patrick Henry's famous speech. Basing his statement on old men's recollections, the flimsiest of evidence, William Wirt in 1817 gave currency to the Henry Myth when he asserted that to Speaker Robinson's charge of treason the young orator retorted: "If *this* be treason, make the most of it!" Magnificent though such a reply appears to-day, it would have been the sheerest folly in 1765 when Patrick Henry was making his initial bid for political leadership. Already, despite his youth, he was too wise in the ways of men to commit the tactical blunder of flinging such a taunt at Speaker Robinson and the gentlemen of the Tidewater. A conciliatory answer was called for; an apology was offered. If the myth misrepresented what Henry said, however, it did not lie in symbolizing the *effect* of the speech, as will be seen in the use to which the Resolutions were put.

On Friday, after Henry, "the very Devil in Politicks—a son of Thunder," and one or two others had left town, Robinson and Randolph worked on some of the more timid Tidewater representatives who had voted for the fifth resolution. The Frenchman reports that returning to the Assembly he "heard very hot debates stil about the Stamp Dutys. The whole house was for Entering [the] resolves in the records, but they Differed much with regard to the Contents or purport thereof." The conservative members succeeded in carrying a motion to expunge the fifth resolution from the Journal. This resolution read:

"*Resolved*, That the General Assembly of this colony have the only sole and exclusive right and power to lay taxes and impositions upon the inhabitants of this colony, and that every attempt to rest such power in any person or persons whatsoever, other than the General Assembly aforesaid, has a manifest tendency to destroy British as well as American freedom." Richard Bland's ideas, John Fleming's rhetoric!

The Assembly completed its business on Friday, and therefore on Saturday morning, Governor Fauquier summoned the

House to the Council Chamber where he gave his assent to the remaining acts. Because of the defiant tone of the burgesses' resolves of May 30 and of his annoyance that "more of the Representatives" had not done "their duty by attending at the end of the Session," he did not deign to deliver the usual speech—"And then his Honour was pleased to dissolve the Assembly."

News of Patrick Henry's incendiary speech in defense of liberty spread over Virginia like wildfire. On June 6 the French traveler took refuge in Johnson's Tavern at Newcastle on the Pamunkey, along with Major Boswell of the Virginia Militia and others, from a twenty-four hour rain, "dureing which we had nothing talked of but the stamp Dutys. The major says freely he'l sooner Die than pay a farthing, and is sure that all his Countrymen will do the Same. There was a great deal said about the Noble Patriot Mr. henery, . . . the whole Inhabitants say publiqly that if the least Injury was offered to him they'd stand by him to the last Drop of their blood." Soon such a moderate as Colonel George Washington was telling London friends that the Stamp Act *engrosses the conversation of the speculative part of the colonists,** who look upon this unconstitutional method of taxation, as a direful attack on their liberties and loudly exclaim against the violation."

The effect of the action of the House of Burgesses was greater outside the colony than within. The "Virginia Resolves," wrote Governor Francis Bernard of Massachusetts, proved an "alarm Bell to the disaffected." The alert politicians who had recently electrified the Assembly were in no small part responsible for this state of "universal consternation,"

* The italics are mine.

which soon spread beyond the borders of Virginia. They carefully saw to it that copies of the four recorded resolves plus the one expunged and the two withheld were sent to Philadelphia correspondents for use where they would do the most good. From this metropolis they were dispatched by water to Rhode Island, and six of them made their first appearance in print in Samuel Hall's *Newport Mercury* for June 24, 1765. This printer, being under no such pressure from royal officials as Joseph Royle of the *Virginia Gazette*, could publish what he chose. Among the six resolves in the *Mercury*, which were reprinted by the *Boston Gazette* on July 1 and soon thereafter by many other newspapers, were the following:

> *Resolved*, That his Majesty's liege People, the Inhabitants of this Colony, are not bound to yield Obedience to any Law or Ordinance whatever, designed to impose any Taxation whatsoever upon them, other than the Laws or Ordinances of the General Assembly aforesaid.

> *Resolved*, That any Person, who shall, by speaking or writing, assert or maintain, that any Person or Persons other than the General Assembly of this Colony have any Right or Power to impose or lay any Taxation on the People here, shall be deemed an Enemy to his Majesty's Colony.

"Oh! those Virginians are men," declared Oxenbridge Thacher as he lay on his deathbed in Boston, "they are noble spirits."

Although these additional resolutions were immediately branded as spurious, it was too late. Through the columns of Mr. Hall's *Mercury*, the Fleming-Henry junto committed the reluctant Assembly to far more than most of them had ever dreamed of saying. Thus not altogether wittingly or willingly did the Virginia House of Burgesses at Williamsburg take the first major step to set off American resistance to the Stamp Act.

By mid-autumn public indignation over the Stamp Act had run far ahead of official opinion, and its expression could no longer be confined to the forum. While he was in London during the summer, George Mercer, a cadet of the prominent Rappahannock family, was appointed distributor of stamps for the colony. When he landed at Hampton on October 29 he met with very rude treatment by a mob but, on the interposition of several gentlemen, was permitted to make his way to Williamsburg. He arrived at the capital in the evening of October 30, two days before the hated Stamp Act was to go into effect. "Very unluckily" the town was full of people attending the meeting of the General Court. Governor Fauquier was a leading participant in what followed, and the incident is vividly described in his words:

"On Wednesday . . . he [Mercer] came up to town. I then thought proper to go to the coffee house (where I occasionally go). . . . My particular reason for going then was that I might be an eye witness of what did really pass, and not receive it by relation from others. The mercantile people were all assembled as usual. The first word I heard was 'One and all' upon which, as at a word agreed on before between themselves, they all quitted the place to find Colonel Mercer at his father's lodgings where it was known he was. This concourse of people I should call a mob, did I not know that it was chiefly if not altogether composed of gentlemen of property in the colony, some of them at the head of their respective counties, and the merchants of the country whether English, Scotch, or Virginian, for few absented themselves.

"They met Colonel Mercer on the way, just at the Capitol.

There they stop'd and demanded of him an answer whether he would resign or act in this office as Distributor of the Stamps. He said it was an affair of great moment to him, he must consult his friends, and promised to give them an answer at 10 o'clock on Friday morning at that place. This did not satisfy them, and they followed him to the coffee house, in the porch of which I had seated myself with many of the Council and the Speaker, who had posted himself between the crowd and myself. We all received him with the greatest marks of welcome; with which, if one may be allowed to judge by their countenances, they were not well pleased, tho' they remained quiet and were silent. Now and then a voice was heard from the crowd, that Friday was too late, the Act would take place, they would have an answer tomorrow. Several messages were brought to Mr. Mercer by the leading men of the crowd, to whom he constantly answered he had already given an answer and he would have no other extorted from him. After some little time a cry was heard, 'let us rush in.' Upon this we that were on the top of the steps, knowing the advantage our situation gave us to repel those who should attempt to mount them, advanced to the edge of the steps, of which number I was one. I immediately heard a cry, 'See the Governor, take care of him.' Those who were before pushing up the steps immediately fell back, and left a small space between me and them. If your Lordships will not accuse me of vanity I would say that I believe this to be partly owing to the respect they bore to my character and partly to the love they bore my person. After much entreaty of some of his friends, Mr. Mercer was, against his own inclination, prevailed upon to promise them an answer at the Capitol the next evening at five.

"The crowd did not yet disperse; it was growing dark, and

I did not think it safe to leave Mr. Mercer behind me, so I again advanced to the edge of the steps and said aloud I believed no man there would do me any hurt, and turned to Mr. Mercer and told him if he would walk with me through the people I believed I could conduct him safe to my house; and we accordingly walked side by side through the thickest of the people, who did not molest us, tho' there was some little murmurs. By my thus taking him under my protection, I believe I saved him from being insulted at least. When we got home we had much discourse on the subject. He asked me what he should do; in return I asked him whether he was afraid for his life, if he was, it was too tender a point for me to advise him; if not, his honor and interest both demanded he should hold the office; and if that should be his resolution he must not regard the reasonings of his father and brother, two lawyers attending the Court who were both frightened out of their senses for him. He left me that night in a state of uncertainty what part he should act."

"Messengers having been sent into the neighborhood for that purpose," a great crowd of gentlemen, merchants, and others gathered at the Capitol the following day to await Mr. Mercer's appearance at five o'clock to give his answer. He came and promptly read his recantation, was cheered by the crowd, and then retired with some of the gentlemen to a public house where, as he was given an elegant entertainment "the Acclamations of the company were redoubled, drums, French horns, etc., sounding all the while." Every window in Williamsburg was illuminated, and the populace coursed through the streets in holiday mood.

Virginians of all ranks proceeded to defy the Stamp Act. Perhaps as enlightening as any one thing was the advertisement inserted by a most restrained and sedate gentleman in Rind's *Virginia Gazette* of May 16, 1766, before the repeal of the law was known in the colony:

> Loudoun, April 5, 1766.
>
> The Subscriber requests it as a Favour of all his Acquaintances, That they will never take any LETTER directed to him out of the POST-OFFICE, as he is determined never willingly to pay a Farthing of any TAX laid upon this COUNTRY, in an UNCONSTITUTIONAL MANNER.
>
> FRANCIS LIGHTFOOT LEE

Henceforth all members of the Virginia ruling class had a large stake in the cause of the colonies. What began in the Old Dominion as a contest for power within the local gentry was transformed by the "Virginia Resolves" into a flaming issue of world-wide consequences, and ended in 1776 with the Declaration of Independence. Virginians soon became proud of having assumed the lead in resistance to the Stamp Act; they rejoiced that they could force England to back down. As they read in letters and newspapers of the riots against stamp collectors at Boston, Newport, New York, and Wilmington, they assured themselves that matters could be managed better in their colony than in those urban centers where whiggish merchants led the mob in the destruction of property. And events were shortly to bear them out.

Any plans of the Tidewater cabal to recover its lost prestige after the repeal of the Stamp Act were frustrated by the sudden death of Speaker John Robinson on May 10, 1766. Nearly a year before, Governor Fauquier had written to the Board of Trade that he seriously doubted whether the elections to the next Assembly would "fall on cool, reasonable men," and as a consequence he also doubted "whether Mr. Robinson will be re-chosen Speaker," even though "the thousand little flattering attentions which can be scattered from the chair operated as a delicious incense." Robinson's death confirmed suspicions dating back to 1753 that much of his influence "was obtained by indirect methods." Far worse was the discovery that while he was treasurer "the public money was misapplied." He had made loans from the colony's funds to the gentlemen of his circle solely on the security of their personal notes, and his accounts were short £102,000. Many of the beneficiaries of his largess, moreover, failed to come forward and acknowledge their indebtedness. Here was a first-class government scandal.

In May, 1766 some of the "hot Burgesses" invited William Rind from Maryland to establish a newspaper which would not be subservient to the governor. The masthead of Rind's *Virginia Gazette* declared its columns to be "Open to all Parties but Influenced by None," yet its tone definitely reflected insurgent opinion in the House of Burgesses, and Purdie and Dixon, who took over the older "official" *Virginia Gazette* at Royle's death, were forced to take the popular side also, which they stoutly maintained was in the interests of a free press. The upshot of this rivalry was that for the first time the pages of these competing journals revealed to astonished Virginians the political skulduggery that had in other days been confined to the conversations of a few gentlemen.

"Every Thing is become a Matter of heat and Party Faction; every thing is contested; a Spirit of Discontent and Cavill runs through the Colony," Government Fauquier sadly observed to the Board of Trade. The newspapers began to raise the question of the late Speaker's defalcation even before the Assembly met in November. When the session opened it became evident that many of the members who had supported the resolutions against the Stamp Act had been returned; whereas many who had opposed them had failed of re-election. In political terms this meant that the Fleming-Henry-Lee combination was holding its ground. Further proof came when Richard Henry Lee's favorite measure, the separation of the offices of speaker and treasurer, was effected, and Speaker-elect Peyton Randolph, a highly respected moderate of the Old Guard, wisely gave the Piedmont men a much more generous representation on the important committees than had his predecessor.

If the Tidewater clique had any hopes of reversing the trend, all such ideas were shattered when the incidents relative to the mishandling of a murder case were bruited about by the press. Colonel John Chiswell of Williamsburg was the father-in-law of the late Speaker Robinson and was connected with most of the great Tidewater families. In the summer of 1766 he murdered an intoxicated Scottish merchant, named Robert Routledge, in cold blood at Cumberland Court House. Before he could be delivered to the keeper of the colony's prison at Williamsburg to await trial, three judges of the General Court, John Blair, William Byrd III, and Presley Thornton, though the court was not in session, stopped him on his way there and admitted him to bail, "led to it no doubt by Chiswell's connections." The newspapers immediately took up the case, and their accounts "put the country into a ferment." The rank favoritism shown this gentleman-killer led many of the gentry to entertain grave doubts that justice

would be done in this instance where the very judges who
would hear the case had already so flagrantly exercised "an
extra-judicial power." Here again was a chance to point the
finger at the Old Guard leaders, who were involved in this
apparent miscarriage of justice. Suddenly, however, Colonel
Chiswell committed suicide at his house on Francis Street in
Williamsburg, thereby saving his "connections" from embar-
rassment, and tension relaxed.

With Chiswell's death all outstanding differences between
the contending groups in the Virginia aristocracy were elimi-
nated or composed. Richard Henry Lee ("as true a trout as
ever swam, as staunch a hound as ever ran") seems to have
been foremost among those who effected the reconciliation.
Treasurer Robert Carter Nicholas and Speaker Peyton Randolph were men of proved ability, probity, and character, and
acceptable to all factions. So long as they were adequately and
fairly represented on committees and received their share of
the other patronage, the "young and giddy members" were
willing that the more moderate adherents of the old entrenched group should continue in the highest offices and
appear to lead the colony. As Virginia faced England this was
a wise public policy. Actually, however, the initiative in the
struggle with the Mother Country continued to rest with
Patrick Henry, Richard Henry Lee, and their followers.
Agreeing on principles, sharing power in the colony, and
representing one class only—the aristocracy—leaders of both
factions closed the ranks of the gentry after 1766, and, unlike any other colony in America, faced King George in 1775
with a united front which, as earlier, they knew was certain
of unquestioning support from the politically silent common

THE HORSE "AMERICA," THROWING HIS MASTER

A contemporary English cartoon

Courtesy Library of Congress

A SYMBOL OF BRITISH TYRANNY: THE MAGAZINE AT WILLIAMSBURG

Governor Dunmore had the colony's powder removed from this place of safe-keeping on the night of April 20, 1775, thereby precipitating armed rebellion in the Old Dominion

folk of the Old Dominion. This unity explains the seeming paradox of conservative Edmund Pendleton drawing up the resolves of the Assembly instructing the insurgent Richard Henry Lee to propose independence to the Continental Congress in May, 1776.

8

THEY KNEW WHAT THEY WANTED

The Stamp Act shocked Virginians into action. After 1765 the colony joined hands with Massachusetts and led the eleven other colonies down the road to revolution. One may properly ask why did the oldest, most aristocratic, and most loyal of His Majesty's colonies in America revolt? What, to use Jefferson's words, impelled them to the separation?

We have seen the powerful conditioning effect of plantation life upon the training of a ruling aristocracy. Virginia gentlemen were called upon for and actually performed an enormous amount of unpaid service, and a share in politics was as much a part of their lives as the economic paternalism they exercised on the tobacco plantations. They came to consider the difficult art of governing people as their responsibility, and eventually their privilege and their right. It had become a vested interest and any challenge to it they would stoutly resist. For them, the greatest social recognition was political preferment accompanied by deference from below.

Since the seventeenth century the first families of Virginia had presided over the destinies of the colony. In their political capacities they had managed rather well on the whole, for the institutions of the Old Dominion were admirably suited to the genius of its people. They formed a contented society, having no serious undercurrent of unrest to ruffle its calm or to alter its steady habits. In this rule by gentlemen there was much privilege, but there was little of the grand or petty graft of modern times; better, middling, and inferior sorts alike unconsciously accepted the regime as normal. When Virginians thought of old England, as they occasionally did, they glowed with pride in the connection.

A chain of events which occurred between 1752 and 1765 rudely disturbed the complacency of many of this politically sensitive gentry. The unyielding attitude of the Crown authorities toward the governor's instructions and the disallowance of the laws which virtually rendered inoperative the entire legal code of the colony raised the specter of external control. No matter what the theory or what the law, *the fact* was that for a very long time Virginians had been running their own show; this colonial society, along with the other American colonies, had slowly, almost imperceptibly, reached maturity without its own members, and certainly without the Mother Country, realizing that it had come of age.

When Parliament in its infinite unwisdom insisted upon taxing the colonies despite their protests and their inability to pay in coin, Virginians threw down the gauntlet. The Stamp Act brought the threat to colonial liberties to a crisis, revealing, as some thought, a danger even greater than there actually was, for at that moment the colony was in a ferment over the fear of a corrupt aristocracy developing here as in England which might lend itself to influence by the British ministry.

Confronted with this situation, the leaders of the Old Do-

minion drew on their experience and the knowledge they had
gained from the histories and books of law. In eighteenth-
century Europe, politics consisted chiefly in maintaining a
balance of power among contending interests as expressed in
social classes. Not a member of any class, the king alone could
act as arbiter among these groups, because he was above and
beyond such strife.

A trans-Atlantic factor complicated this familiar pattern in
the unique case of Britain and her self-governing colonies. By
1759 many Virginians had come to believe that in its own
sphere, their Assembly was the equal, the peer, of the British
Parliament; that their aristocrats stood on the same plane of
equality with the ruling class of the British Isles; that their
colony was the king's fifth or Old Dominion, not a part of
his realm of England, and that they owed allegiance only to
the Crown.

With great sagacity and a striking singleness of purpose, the
gentlemen of Virginia stubbornly insisted upon their right to
determine the conditions under which they would live in their
own country. Repeatedly they warned their fellowmen
against complacency. "The tricks of state are best managed
by those that are suspected least, and the most unlikely engines
are often used to bring about the greatest finesse," exclaimed
"A Lover of Liberty" in Rind's *Virginia Gazette*. No "Gentleman," the great English philosopher John Locke had taught,
can honorably submit to slavery, and since Americans are sons
of Britons, this writer continued, "I am persuaded that no
Gentlemen can possibly entertain a thought so humiliating
and base." In England "wicked Ministers and corrupt lawyers
are suffered to unhinge the constitution and break down the
palladium of their property," but though they may "enslave

the people" there, they must not be permitted to do so here.

Thanks to the events of 1765-1766, there was as yet no challenge to the rule of gentlemen in Virginia. Unlike Pennsylvania and New York where popular leaders taught the people about the "dangers of an inconvenient aristocracy," and where social revolt from below proved as great a threat as the Mother Country, Virginia's planter-statesmen had no fear of the "mob" such as paralyzed Gouverneur Morris. Democracy was as yet unborn; aristocracy was still in the saddle and still virile. In fact it produced a set of leaders and political thinkers whose talents and devotion to principles astounded the world. These first gentlemen of Virginia were sure of themselves; they knew what they wanted.

The debate on Patrick Henry's resolutions had made the most profound impression upon an eager young man of twenty-two who had stood listening outside the door. Soon Thomas Jefferson was hard at work reading and pondering upon the relationship between Virginia and the Mother Country. The repeal of the Stamp Act in 1766 seemed a happy solution to most, but Jefferson and his fellow Virginians took the Declaratory Act seriously when it asserted in sweeping terms the power of king and Parliament to "make laws and statutes of sufficient force and validity to bind the colonies in all cases whatsoever." He and a few others like George Mason and the Lees (Richard Henry, Francis Lightfoot, William, and Arthur) now found themselves forced into a consideration of the whole question of government. Virginia leaders watched every move of King George and his ministers, whether in England or America. Through the efforts of Arthur Lee in London they were kept well informed of the struggle of John Wilkes and his followers for "liberty," for this contest seemed to them to be but a phase of their own cause, and the colony's press persistently drove this home to its readers.

Since Virginians had seen the Stamp Act applied to America and then the military used against the supporters of Wilkes at the massacre of St. George's Fields in London, they knew in their hearts that George III was no longer a patriot king; he had ceased to be the arbiter of his people by becoming a partisan in his own right. This conclusion was borne in on them as the Townshend Acts were forced upon the colonists, and so they entered into nonimportation agreements to nullify the effects of the duties. When, after an illusory calm in the early seventies, they saw their sister colony of Massachusetts faced with the tyranny of the "Intollerable Acts," a group of burgesses met in the Raleigh Tavern in Williamsburg and sent out a call for a congress of all the colonies to concert on measures for the support of the Bostonians. What Virginians had most feared had now come true.

In 1774 when Parliament sought to punish Massachusetts for dumping tea overboard, Thomas Jefferson gave in his *Summary View of the Rights of British America* final expression to the theories first advanced by Richard Bland in 1753, by stating unconditionally that "the true ground on which we declare these acts void is, that the British Parliament has no right to exercise authority over us," and that "experience confirms the propriety of those political principles, which exempt us from the jurisdiction of the British Parliament."

As King George, through his ministers, employed force to coerce the colonists and allowed his troops to burn American towns, Virginia maintained that he had degenerated into a tyrant. Throughout history aristocracies have been the greatest enemies of kingship, and that of Virginia was to deal monarchy the greatest blow it had ever suffered. Their equality and status questioned, even threatened, the now united gentry became radicals, gentlemen revolutionists, and reluctantly but irrevocably reached the decision that if they were to preserve their liberties and retain control of their own government, monarchy must go.

Virginians were conservative revolutionists in that they revolted to preserve what they had; they were radicals in that they resurrected the republican, antimonarchial theories of the seventeenth century to justify their action. Theirs was not a democratic uprising. It was rebellion against a bad king and an even worse system in his own realm, quite as much as against what he was attempting to do over here. Having already denied Parliament's competence to legislate for the colonies in any case whatsoever, it only remained, when independence was decided upon, to issue to "a candid world" a bill of particulars against George III. In his proposed constitution for Virginia, drawn up in June, 1776, Jefferson stated with all the magnificent contempt of an aroused aristocrat that "Whereas George Guelf king of Britain and Ireland and Elector of Hanover, heretofore entrusted with the exercise of the kingly office in this government had endeavored to pervert the same into a detestable and insupportable tyranny," therefore *"Guelf has forfeited the kingly office,"** and is "by the authority of the people" hereby deposed from it.

* * *

When in 1780 the capital of Virginia was moved from Williamsburg to Richmond, aristocracy and the rule of the planter-gentlemen still held sway. One of them, Thomas Jef-

* The italics are mine.

ferson, jarred by the Stamp Act into an analysis of England's injustice to the colonies, had proceeded logically to a consideration of mankind's injustice to man. To him, entrenched power seemed as wrong in Virginia as it was everywhere else, and in the Declaration of Independence he had boldly asserted that all governments exist to ensure the happiness and safety of their peoples. In time he succeeded in persuading enough gentlemen of the wrongness of the inequalities existing in the Old Dominion to enable him to push through a program of reform. He erected this program on the solid foundations of George Mason's great Bill of Rights which was adopted by the General Convention in the Capitol at Williamsburg on June 12, 1776—but that is another story.

Democracy—that for which we contend today—did not spring full blown from a single historical event. No one locality in America can rightfully claim to be the "Cradle of Democracy." The political history of eighteenth-century Virginia is the chronicle of the development of self-government by a special, privileged class, an able, responsible class, who gradually came to hold republican theories and, in the end, disposed of kings. This was an accomplishment of the greatest magnitude.

For eighty years the capital of the colony of Virginia was the scene of activities which cleared away the rubbish of feudalism and monarchy, without which the great development of democracy in the nineteenth and twentieth centuries could never have taken place. Few communities in any age have witnessed more far-reaching political happenings than this tiny seat of empire.

This is the lesson of Williamsburg.

A NOTE ON THE SOURCES

Books on the subjects treated in this essay are few, and, consequently, it was written almost exclusively from the sources themselves. Of first importance for any understanding of this period of Virginia's history are the three newspapers, each called the *Virginia Gazette*, published at Williamsburg between 1750 and 1779; the *Legislative Journals of the Council of the Colony of Virginia*; and the *Journals of the House of Burgesses of Virginia*. An unpublished doctoral dissertation in the Princeton University Library (by J. Kimbrough Owen) deals thoroughly with the parish, and Albert O. Porter's *County Government in Virginia* (1947) covers its subject. Robert Munford, "The Candidates; or, The Humours of a Virginia Election," *William and Mary Quarterly*, third series, 5 (1949), 217-57, is a minor classic. The two articles by Stanley M. Pargellis in the *William and Mary Quarterly*, second series, 7 (1927), provide a thorough description of the procedure of the House of Burgesses. *The Life of the Reverend Devereux Jarratt* (1806) is one of those rare books that offer insight into the important question of social distinctions. The writings of Richard Bland, as indicated in the text, are of primary significance, as are the *Letters* of Richard Henry Lee and his brother William (1891). In his admirable *Edmund Pendleton* (1952), David J. Mays treats the affair of Speaker Robinson's accounts definitively, and provides a charming description of the legal profession. My discussion of the Stamp Act resolutions by the House of Burgesses follows closely the "History of Virginia" by Edmund Randolph, which is still in manuscript in the Virginia Historical Society at Richmond. The most recent and standard account of this momentous subject is by Edmund and Helen Morgan, *The Stamp Act Crisis* (1953); in presenting a somewhat varying story, they do not appear to have used the Randolph version, which I value because its author was very close to the actual happenings.

Lavish use has been made of the writings of travelers, of which those by Thomas Anburey, Nicholas Cresswell, the Reverend Andrew Burnaby, the Marquis de Chastellux, Philip Vickers Fithian, Hugh Jones, Josiah Quincy, Jr., Lt. William Feltman, Lord Adam Gordon, the Duc de la Rochefoucauld-Liancourt, and J. D. Schoepf are the best known and most easily attainable in large libraries. Particular attention should be paid to the "Journal of a French Traveller in the American Colonies," *American Historical Review*, 26 (1921), 726-47; 27 (1922), 70-89, the pertinent parts of which are printed with other accounts, "in ascending versions . . . to show how tradition is made," by S. E. Morison, *Sources and Documents Illustrating the American Revolution* (1923), to which Edmund Randolph's version ought to be appended. The growth of antimonarchical sentiment is traced by Stella F. Duff in "The Case Against the King," *William and Mary Quarterly*, third series, 6 (1949), 383-97.

SUGGESTIONS FOR FURTHER READING

In *Virginians at Home*, the second volume of this *Williamsburg in America Series*, Edmund S. Morgan presents in a lively manner the family life of the Old Dominion. Two volumes in the *Williamsburg Restoration Historical Studies* provide an intimate picture of life on one of the great eighteenth-century plantations: Louis Morton's *Robert Carter of Nomini Hall* (1941), and H. D. Farish's edition of Philip Fithian's charming *Diary* (1943; 1957). The most satisfactory biography of a great leader is David Mays' *Edmund Pendleton*; Burton J. Hendrick's *The Lees of Virginia* is written with distinction. The first volume of Robert D. Meade's *Patrick Henry* (1957) deals with the Stamp Act; but the shrewd estimate in Irving Brant's *James Madison: The Virginia Revolutionist* (1941) is still essential for Henry's role. The gentry of the Old Dominion are assessed in *Myths and Realities: Societies of the Colonial South* (1953), by Carl Bridenbaugh, who also discusses the artisans in *The Colonial Craftsman* (1950). The late Charles S. Sydnor's *Gentlemen Freeholders* (1952) is, in a sense, a sequel to the present volume, carrying the story down to 1800. For the facts of the revolutionary movement, there is an excellent study by Charles R. Lingley, *The Transition in Virginia from Colony to Commonwealth* (1910); and Rutherfoord Goodwin genially supplies much useful data in *A Brief & True Report Concerning Williamsburg in Virginia* (1940).

INDEX

This new edition of

SEAT OF EMPIRE

*was composed and printed by
the William Byrd Press, Inc., in 1958 for Colonial
Williamsburg, Williamsburg, Virginia. The type used
is Janson. The paper is Perkins & Squier Antique
Wove made by the Glatfelter Paper Company. Binding
was by the Russell Rutter Company, Inc., New York.
The book was designed by Richard J. Stinely.*

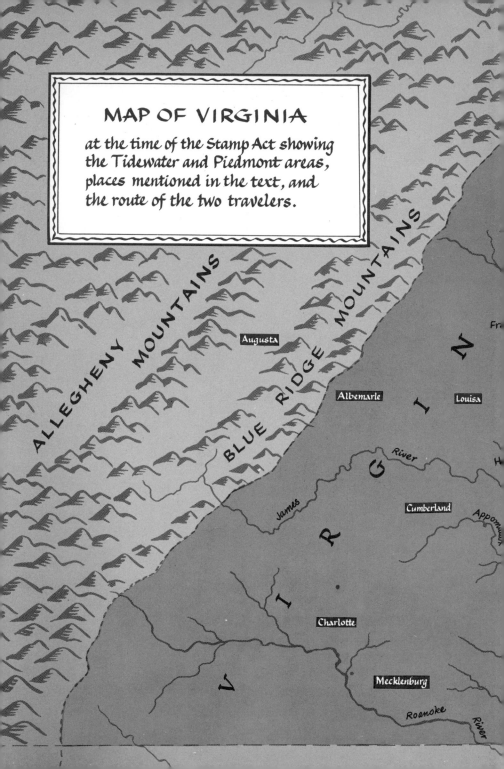

MAP OF VIRGINIA

at the time of the Stamp Act showing
the Tidewater and Piedmont areas,
places mentioned in the text, and
the route of the two travelers.

ALLEGHENY MOUNTAINS

BLUE RIDGE MOUNTAINS

Augusta

Albemarle

Louisa

River

James

Cumberland

Appomattox

V I R G I N

Charlotte

Mecklenburg

Roanoke

River

Fr